PRAISE FOR P

MW00576230

"Our stories matter. They in_____ _____ ____ ___ ____ ____ in this book, Mary Dowell, a lifelong teacher and mentor, shares a collection of stories to buoy you, to lift you and to help you face your own difficulty in the same way that these brave and amazing women have. Pick it up when you need to be brave. Read a chapter when you need a lift. These women have been where you are, and they show us a way out and through."
— Rebecca Ryan, Founder, NEXT Generation Consulting, Inc.

"In a warm and engaging style, Mary Dowell presents a book that would be of interest to all women seeking to become leaders in their lives and especially in their careers. The case studies will inspire young women, all too many of whom do not perceive the challenges that lie ahead; for those in mid-career, the book will be a reminder that they are not alone, and that success is within reach; and for those of us at the end of our careers, we will be able to reflect on all that we accomplished, sometimes against what seemed insurmountable obstacles. This book is a wonderful journey for all women who believe that there is always a pathway to success."
— Mary J. Meehan, PhD, President, Alverno College

"Playing Through the Fence *makes a compelling statement through the impact of life stories from a diverse group of women leaders who overcome and transform obstacles into opportunities. Dowell's story and perspective threads their experiences together with facts and practical suggestions. She gives voice to how they each took charge of their lives and careers with courage and conviction."*
—Dr. Kathleen H. Kueht, Founder & CEO, CREACTION Global Consulting

"Inspiring and thought provoking—a must-read for anyone aspiring to maximize their full potential."
— Ralph Hollmon, President & CEO, Milwaukee Urban League

"A tender and thoughtful story of living, learning and loving persistently in an era of –isms, 'Playing Through the Fence' should prove an approachable and inspiring tool for emerging leaders wanting to rise above external forces that may hold them back."
—Dr. Magda G. Peck, ScD, Founder/Principal, MP3 Health Group

"As a millennial woman with goals to build an impactful career, 'Playing Through the Fence' has inspired me to continue the legacy of female pioneers, who tirelessly blazed the trail for all of us, by trusting my instinct, seeking wisdom and holding onto persistence."
—Hailey E. Nenonen, Strategic Program Manager, Tea Leaves Health

"The way in which Mary Dowell connects her childhood experience of friendship, tarnished and interrupted by the fence of racism, to the walls that keep bigotry and sexism alive in corporate America, is both touching and provocative. This powerful book of stories from 19 women, who overcame 'in spite of,' provides encouragement to all."
— Eve M. Hall, Ph.D., President & CEO,
African American Chamber of Commerce of Wisconsin

"Innocence comes to stand or sit next to the fence for the willful refusal of all barriers and borders. The obstacles placed on society are based upon race, gender and class, and these powerful experiences of women collectively question inequities, unfairness, unethical and plainly wrong behaviors for the simple reasoning of the color of their skin, gender or social class. There is strength in numbers, and the efforts of these women help to free the opportunity for generations to follow."
—Marie L. O'Brien, President & CEO, Enterforce, Inc.

Playing Through the Fence

Stories from 19 Women
Who Challenged Stereotypes,
Prejudice and Other Barriers
to Achieve Career Success

All My Best!

[signature]

Playing Through the Fence

Stories from 19 Women
Who Challenged Stereotypes,
Prejudice and Other Barriers
to Achieve Career Success

Mary J. Dowell

HenschelHAUS Publishing, Inc.
Milwaukee, Wisconsin

Published by
HenschelHAUS Publishing, Inc.
www.henschelhausbooks.com

ISBN: 978159598-474-6
E-ISBN: 978159598-475-3
LCCN: 2016946902

Publisher's Cataloging-In-Publication Data
(Prepared by The Donohue Group, Inc.)

Names: Dowell, Mary J.
Title: Playing through the fence : stories from 19 women who challenged stereotypes, prejudice and other barriers to achieve career success / Mary J. Dowell.
Description: Milwaukee, Wisconsin : HenschelHAUS Publishing, Inc., [2016]
Identifiers: LCCN 2016946902 | ISBN 978-1-59598-474-6 |
   ISBN 978-1-59598-475-3 (ebook)
Subjects: LCSH: Dowell, Mary J. | Glass ceiling (Employment discrimination) | Sex discrimination against women. | Women executives. | Leadership in women. | Opportunity. | Success in business.
Classification: LCC HD6060 .D69 2016 (print) | LCC HD6060 (ebook) | DDC 331.4133--dc23

Printed in the United States of America

*This book is dedicated to
all those who have faced adversity
and triumphed.*

Table of Contents

About this Book

Playing Through the Fence is part memoir, part self-help for emerging leaders or anyone seeking inspiration while facing obstacles on his or her career journey. Nineteen women share powerful reflections of fortitude and accomplishments in their lives and careers, sometimes against what seemed like impossible odds, as they challenged barriers on their paths to success.

A metaphor for these barriers, "The Fence" represents the crossroads where struggle meets opportunity. The stories shared by these women are snapshots in time when they chose the path of opportunity. We are reminded that we are not alone, and that success, though sometimes appearing elusive, is always within reach.

Career titles of individuals have been omitted because careers have changed over time (and during the course of writing this book). Names have been changed to maintain the anonymity of individuals in their stories.

Acknowledgments

A number of individuals have generously provided support during the writing of this book. I am personally grateful to the admirable women listed below who accepted my invitation to recount their inspirational struggles, accomplishments, dissatisfaction and optimism that got them where they are today: Christina Allen, Maggie Beckley, Sheree Dallas Branch, Angela Brooks, Maria Cadenas, Cheryl Carron, Tina Chang, Faithe Colas, Debra Crawford, Cristy Garcia-Thomas, Margaret Henningsen, Bernell Hooker, Joan Kessler, Maria Monreal-Cameron, Kimberley Noon, Deloris Sims, Becky Trochinski and Shanon Vuckovic.

I also want to thank my husband, John, and our daughters, Juvonda Dowell-Dulin and LaTonya Dowell-Jacobs, who provided support and understanding throughout this effort. I appreciate their patience, encouragement, understanding, and above all, their unwavering love.

Although they have passed on, I'd like to thank my parents, Eugene and Lacey Cabknor, for continuing to be an inspiration to my siblings and me. They instilled in us the belief that our dreams could become realities and that we could accomplish our hearts' desires as long as we were willing to work for it.

And finally, I would like to thank my editor, Lesley DeMartini, who has been a friend, mentor, and advisor on the writing of this book.

Foreword

Every now and then a book comes along that reframes a long-standing issue in a way that leaves readers feeling refreshed, reassured and quietly happy. *Playing Through the Fence* by Mary J. Dowell takes an upfront and personal look at the obstacles and challenges faced by a cast of 19 characters, each of whom tells a story of triumph.

This is not a book of clichés or larger-than-life superwomen. It is a collection of personal stories that expose gritty realities and meets them with heart and determination that is bolstered by love and support from people who believed in them. In each case, a by-product of struggle is emotional enrichment. Mary's voice is heard throughout the book, reminding us "where there is obstacle, there is opportunity." She looks back on her own journey of challenge, disappointment, growth and success with a depth of wisdom that comes with time.

Her grateful attitude and graceful hand transforms this medley of stories into an anthem of strength, beauty and triumph that is accessible and eminently relatable not only to women of all ages and stages of development, but to every human being who has faced dismissal. A foundational concept that rings throughout the book is also a call to action: "Crisis is a moment to decide; an opportunity to grow."

In my work with thousands of individuals over several decades, this truth separates people who grow from those who become discouraged and give up. When you decide to grow, you begin a process of enlarging your experience, sharpening your mind and creating new possibility. This book offers reassurance that your effort, however painful or disappointing in the moment, is worthwhile. You are worth the struggle to flourish and grow. Then, having overcome life's toughest challenges, you are beautifully equipped to lend a hand of support to others looking for a reason to go on.

Mary Dowell's journey is a testament to this truth and a gift of love for generations to come.

Susan A. Marshall
Founder, Backbone Institute, LLC
Author of:
How to Grow a Backbone
Life—Be In It
Of Beauty and Substance: A Backbone Guide for Women

Preface

I guess you could say I'm a true southern girl, having been born in Alabama and raised in the rolling hills of Tennessee. I have a passion for a mild southern breeze on my face, going fishing with my dad on a summer evening and a tall glass of sweet tea.

I grew up with my mom, dad and five siblings. Our family size was not unusual in those days, as almost everyone came from big families—some much larger than ours. Growing up with so many siblings meant there was always someone to play with. I was never lonely or bored.

My parents were blue-collar workers. Dad worked for the city water works department, and Mom worked in a factory. We lived in a predominately black neighborhood, with the exception of one white family and one grocery store owner, whose business operated in the heart of the neighborhood.

The store owner's name was Mr. Clark. My siblings and I visited his store often, selling him our empty soda bottles to buy candy. Mr. Clark was a friendly, heavy-set man with thinning hair and a vibrant laugh that showed spaces where teeth had once been. Looking back, I think he must have had sinus problems because he coughed a lot and was always clearing his throat. He allowed us to meander up and down the food aisles of the store without questioning our intent or rushing us to move along. I think Mr. Clark was genuinely content being part of the neighborhood and considered the people who resided there true neighbors.

I never felt that my family was any different than anyone else's, because our lifestyle was so closely aligned with most of the people we knew. It was said at some point that we were poor, but I never felt poor. We were raised in the same basic, earthy way my parents had been, and we did things the same way our neighbors did them—right down to our bountiful vegetable garden. For fun, we frequently went to the Dairy Queen for ice cream and to the movie theater on Saturdays.

Sundays were always reserved for church, and we spent most of the day there—with morning Sunday school class, 10:45 service, an evening program and a night service. My father and mother both had strong religious backgrounds and assured us that they had plans to enter Heaven when it was time. I believe that keeping church as an integral part of our lives was their way of ensuring their children would be joining them.

My mother had to be organized to manage six children, and she took a lot of pride in doing so. She made sure we always had clean clothes, and though many of them were hand-me-downs, we could always count on getting new clothes every Easter and Christmas. She prepared a full, hot breakfast for all six of us every morning, and she strongly believed that children should have milk every day—or at least a tall glass for breakfast. She would pack each of us a lunch for school, and we each received four pennies to buy a carton of milk. With dinner, we drank Kool-Aid.

There was, however, one thing that set us apart from the neighborhood: My parents raised chickens in our backyard. So while we always had ample meat to eat, chicken was especially plentiful—and of course lots of eggs. Unfortunately, this did not help any of us kids with our popularity. We were often the brunt of many chicken jokes.

Our neighborhood was open and friendly. Everyone knew each other and each other's children. It was a big informal family, bound by certain commonalities: working parents, some with multiple jobs, kids going to the same schools, etc. The families looked out for one another. If someone saw one of my siblings or me doing something we shouldn't have been doing, they would not hesitate for one second to inform my parents.

All the houses in our neighborhood were constructed of wood. All, that is, except one. The house next door was made of large gray stone, and it was home to the only white family.

I don't remember exactly when the Watsons moved in, but I believe I was eight or nine. Their family consisted of two grandparents, two parents, and Jane—a girl about my age.

Jane was short in stature, with a slight build and brown eyes. I was taller and very slim. She had light brown hair that she was always pulling back from her face. I wore my hair in three braids— one on top and one on each side, which were sometimes adorned with small bow-shaped barrettes. I always had a sibling or two to play with, but Jane was an only child—and it quickly became apparent, as we played in our own backyards, that she was eager to have someone to play with. For a short time we played separately, each on our own side of the tattered, wire fence that separated our properties. But we were quickly drawn to that fence, and to each other, and soon became fast friends and inseparable playmates.

The fence was about six feet high, with holes that varied in size and places where it was in severe disrepair. We began to play along it, each staying on our own properties but taking advantage of the holes that provided access to each other and each other's toys. Above us hovered a massive oak tree, rooted in Jane's yard, which stood at least 80 feet tall. Its huge branches swayed in the southern breeze and graciously provided shade during our playtime through the fence, especially during the heat of the summer.

As our friendship grew, so did the amount of time we spent along the fence. What we were playing on any given day determined where along the fence we positioned our stools of upside-down buckets. If we were playing with dolls, we needed to be at a spot where the dolls could fit through easily in order to share them with each other. If we were having a tea party, the hole didn't need to be as large—just big enough for a tiny cup of make-believe tea to fit through. A couple of the holes were large enough for either of us to pass through, but neither Jane nor I ever did. We knew our boundaries. I was black and Jane was white. Instinctively (and because of frequent reminders), we knew not to cross that line—so we didn't. Neither of us wanted to risk our ability to play together or be friends.

Jane's mother was a kind woman, and both our mothers were open to us playing together—but again, only through the fence. Jane's grandparents, however, were not as supportive. As I recall, her grandfather never really talked to us at all—and I never said anything to him. Jane's grandmother would only exchange words with my mother (and few at that) when they both happened to be in their yards at the same time. Jane's mother always had a bright, friendly smile, and she and my mother talked often—but, like us, always through the fence.

I only saw the inside of Jane's house once, when her grandmother suffered a massive heart attack and her family cried out for my mother to help. I ran beside my mother and entered the house. My first thought was how incredibly similar it looked to our house—curtains, chairs, throws on the sofa. It all felt very familiar.

When I entered the room where all the commotion was, I saw Jane's grandmother lying on the floor. She was motionless. Jane's father was bent over her, trying to give her mouth-to-mouth resuscitation. She continued to lie there, without any signs of life. Jane and I looked at each other with wide-eyed astonishment. I didn't know what to do and dared not say a word. Jane and I inched our way to each other and locked arms, something we never had an opportunity to do and yet somehow felt natural and familiar. The ambulance arrived and carried Jane's grandmother away. She never regained consciousness.

One might think that the painful experience we shared that day might have evoked a closer relationship between our two families, but it didn't. Jane attended her grandmother's funeral; my family sent flowers. Like the fence that separated us, the boundaries were back up—and life between our families remained the same as they were before. Jane and I never spoke about the incident or her sadness. She was very close to her grandmother, and while I know she must have missed her terribly, it was not a conversation to be shared between us. This was part of the unwritten rules by which we lived.

I don't remember exactly when Jane's family moved away, but I will always have a special place in my heart for her. Many decades later, I reflect not only on my time with her, but also on the fence, the tree, and the memories that helped to shape the person I later became. In the context of dolls and tea, the fence was merely a passage to our play. It wasn't until many years later that I understood the power it represented in my life.

My climb in corporate America evolved from an entry-level secretary to the vice president of global community relations for a Fortune 500 company—but the journey was not without its challenges. Each obstacle I encountered presented me with its own type of fence—and none came with dolls or tea. Instead, those obstacles were the dark side of what the fence represented for me, resulting in years of struggle against racism and sexism. However, that fence also symbolized opportunity. I seized many opportunities and reaped great benefits in my career and in my life.

The fence from my childhood is a symbolic memory for me. It's a place where we, as women, have often found ourselves at different stages in our lives and careers—at a crossroads between what is and what should be. A place of choice—to accept the status quo, or to inspire change.

Along my career path, I have met some incredible women with incredible stories. Whether becoming the CEO of their own company or securing a seat at the corporate table, they too encountered unique challenges and opportunities along the way and broke through fences of their own. While the backgrounds, struggles and successes expressed in these stories are very different, what they all have in common is, and continues to be, the magic bullet for their success. This commonality is their inner strength—their intestinal fortitude to keep putting one foot in front of the other—combined with such traits as perseverance, determination, honesty and faith—that made their individual successes possible.

These women continue to inspire me—and I have the utmost admiration and respect for their accomplishments. I thank them for sharing their stories that reflect a particular time along their journeys. It is my hope that you find inspiration in these stories as well and that they inspire you to overcome obstacles in your own careers and personal lives.

I am constantly reminded that where there is obstacle, there is opportunity. Expectations can be exceeded despite incredible opposition. Glass ceilings can be broken, brick walls can be demolished, and fences can be hurdled, bulldozed or torn apart—with rewards far more fulfilling than an empty cup of tea.

I thank these women for their support, their leadership and their commitment to themselves. May you all continue to do great work and inspire great change.

Mary J. Dowell

Chapter One
A Moment to Decide
Choosing to Persevere

"Making your mark on the world is hard. If it were easy,
everybody would do it. But it's not. It takes patience,
it takes commitment, and it comes with plenty of failure along
the way. The real test is not whether you avoid this failure,
because you won't. It's whether you let it harden or shame
you into inaction, or whether you learn from it; whether
you choose to persevere."
— Barack Obama, 44th President of the United States

MARY

The election of Barack Obama as the first African-American president was triumphant not only for the achievement it was, but for the statement it made: Success and change are not just possible—but within reach.

Unfortunately, for many, obstacles in the way of success are too challenging. Racism, sexism and discrimination of any kind in the workplace can be devastating experiences. Today's professional world is full of all types of people of varying race, gender, sexual orientation and physical abilities. From my own experiences as an African-American working woman, I've learned when to stay and when to leave professional environments that come with a side of discrimination, however subtle. I don't advocate running away from issues of prejudice; in fact, I recommend doing whatever

1

possible to find resolution—though sometimes this becomes far easier said than done.

Many years ago, working as a senior secretary in the banking industry, I felt confident I was getting very close to my ultimate goal of becoming an executive secretary. I worked for a vice president who was Hispanic, whom I'll call Antonio. I also reported to another VP, in the same office, who was Caucasian. I'll call him Mark. Reporting to two vice presidents kept me extremely busy. I enjoyed my job and worked hard, always taking pride in being very professional and having a strong work ethic.

Being the only woman of color in the entire office made me very aware of my surroundings, but the other women were very pleasant and treated me in a professional manner. Mark did the same, often complimenting my work. However, I soon began to sense negative feelings coming from Antonio.

No matter how pleasant I was or how detailed and responsive I was to my work, Antonio never seemed pleased with me. While he was never verbally critical of my work—in fact, he never discussed my work with me at all—his silence spoke volumes to me. Soon it became very apparent that Antonio was not happy with me as his assistant.

Frequently, Antonio would ask me why I chose to work. He said he didn't understand why I wasn't staying at home, as I had a husband who had a good job. Each time he asked me, I would answer the same way: that I enjoyed being in the workforce and that I particularly enjoyed working at the senior secretary level.

I noticed that he didn't treat the other women in the office this way, nor did I ever hear him question any of them about their decisions to work. Eventually I gathered by his questions and behavior that Antonio couldn't get over the fact that I didn't look like the other secretaries. He appeared to not be comfortable having a person of color in the office—even being of color himself. This was difficult for me, as no matter what I did to demonstrate my credentials as a top-notch secretary, it never seemed to make him happy or accepting of me.

I continued to work for Antonio for several months, feeling worse with the passing of each, until an incident one day made it clear this arrangement wasn't going to work out for either of us.

It had started to rain, and Antonio came out of his office, tossed his keys on my desk, and told me to go roll up the windows in his car. He walked back to his office, and I just sat there. I didn't know what to do. Finally, I stood up and walked to the window. It was pouring. I had no umbrella, nor did he offer me one. I walked slowly back to my desk and sat down, feeling numb and bewildered. I couldn't get myself to do it.

A few moments later, he returned. He looked at his keys, still where he'd tossed them, and asked me if I had rolled up his windows. With my heart pounding, I shook my head no, not able to offer any excuse. I felt a horrible dread, knowing in that moment my time in that office was limited. He picked up the keys and went back into his office. He did not go out to roll up his own windows, nor did he say anything else to me about it. Was it a test to see how far he could push me? Or how badly I wanted my job? Whatever the reason, things didn't get better after that.

Other subtleties continued over the next several months. As the pressures continued to escalate, I eventually, and reluctantly, gave my notice. On my last day of work, Antonio called me into his office. He stared me coldly in the eyes and told me good luck, and then he said, "You know, you are a good entry-level secretary—but you will never be skilled enough to be an executive secretary." Hurt, embarrassed and confused, I knew I could manage only a few words out of my trembling lips without crying. I lifted my eyes to his and said, "I will be an executive secretary."

Three months later, I secured a position at a Fortune 500 company as an executive secretary. During my tenure, I was promoted to a staff recruiter in human resources, and later to an HR manager.

My job at the bank taught me that not all jobs are the right ones. We can't be all things to all people. And sexism and racism, even when very subtle, sometimes cannot be overcome. For me, it meant letting go and allowing the next phase in my career to begin.

* * * * * * * *

MARIA CADENAS

When I look at my life, I don't focus as much on the obstacles that I've overcome as I do on the lessons that I've learned. For me, it's all about using my life experiences in order to move forward, both personally and professionally.

One of the greatest lessons I've learned is about the importance of information and access to it through mentors. For example, if you are of college age but no one in your family or group of friends has attended college, you'll lack information about the whole process—and as a result, you might miss the opportunity for yourself. Similarly, when you're starting out in your career, it is crucial that you have a mentor to guide you through.

A Moment to Decide—Choosing to Persevere

Mentors have played an integral role in my life. Most of my mentors have been white women in positions of power who were willing to take the time to guide me to and through opportunities that I wouldn't have known about otherwise. They helped me build my career by answering questions about what made a good manager and what a good professional acted and looked like. They were role models to me, and those women—and, yes, a few men who saw the value of female leadership—taught me the power of connecting with others.

During college, I was an intern for a large insurance company and was under the supervision of various managers—all of whom happened to be women. Later when I started as a consultant for a Fortune 500 management consulting firm, I also worked for women. Working under so many female leaders early on helped me visualize what kind of leader I wanted to become: one who listens to her employees, one who has a group approach to management, and one who is willing to adapt to changing situations in a professional manner without becoming frantic.

My mentors helped me understand the value of paying it forward. I acknowledge that my success is due in great part to many women, especially women of color, and I want to help the next generation. I want to help them learn, as I did, about the power of communication and good listening. In my case, as a Latina and a lesbian, I needed to figure out how to communicate past the stereotypes that most people carry into boardrooms and committee meetings. With the help of my mentors, I learned to move beyond my gut reactions to what I perceived as insensitive comments and have the patience to explain my perspective. I learned that in order to engage in valuable dialogue, I must establish boundaries and my own professional principles while also acknowledging the experiences and beliefs of my coworkers or business associates—and to accept that sometimes there's a learning curve.

Playing Through the Fence

Early on in my career, I also learned about the importance of self-branding. Everybody talks about brands for companies and organizations, but if you really want to be perceived as a professional woman, you must brand yourself and represent your brand at all times. If you aim to be perceived as a driven person who always gives 150 percent and is an optimistic, fearless, responsible, trustworthy team player, then you must be true to those values. You cannot slide, even when it's difficult. Today, as the director of a community foundation that focuses on the gay and lesbian community, there is a level of trustworthiness that is expected from me. I cannot do anything to jeopardize that part of my brand. I must remain true to the person I want to be: a hardworking, trustworthy, honest person who has a real commitment to the community I live in. I can't compromise that for a second, or it will come back to me.

From your first internship or volunteer job and throughout your career, you accumulate experiences that shape who you are as a professional, and this becomes your personal brand. You have to take care of that brand, because you can waste it very quickly. And for women of color, who are judged on a much harsher scale, I've learned that it's even more important.

Another lesson: Never underestimate the power of cheerleaders. Everybody needs people who offer support in a constructive way, who are willing to tell you when you are in the wrong and who can guide you through difficult situations. These people don't have to be in the same company or industry that you're in. They can be your mentors, or role models, or even your family or friends. The bottom line is that when you have a support system, you are never standing alone, and when you encounter difficult times, you'll be able to surround yourself with people who will cheer you on.

In our professional lives, we encounter barriers both big and small. When I was just starting my career, I put a picture of my life partner on my desk. A client questioned whether that was a good idea, putting my lesbianism out there for the world to see. It was a difficult discussion, but we moved forward. That was a small one.

A bigger, lifelong barrier has been dealing with racism. I was in elementary school when my family immigrated to the United States from Mexico, and I was often called a "wetback" and a "spic." It was shocking. I had never experienced racism before, but I had to move on. I learned English and left behind those who were not strengthening me.

In my professional life, I've encountered co-workers who haven't been my supporters or cheerleaders. There's no point in wasting energy with these kinds of people. Move on and find those who will build you up and help you out. Don't waste your time and talents fighting battles that aren't worth it.

But perhaps the biggest lesson I've learned is about the importance of giving back. When I was at the management consulting firm, I wanted to get involved in community work. But because I was working 12 hours a day in a city that wasn't my own, that was a difficult task. After creating some dialogue in my office, I connected with some other employees who were interested in community involvement, and we created a committee. We discovered a local community need for Spanish information and brochures, and we took on the project. Never be afraid to speak up and remember that giving to others is also giving to yourself.

When I started working at a well-known LGBT foundation, one of my first accomplishments was to create an internship program. Seventy percent of my interns have been young women and 50 percent have been women of color. That has been purely coincidental, not a targeted effort, but it has allowed me to open doors to women who might not have known about philanthropy or not-for-profit career opportunities otherwise.

At the foundation, we are committed to the need for social change while understanding that we are all connected. There are systems that discriminate against certain classes of people—whether they're gay, black, Latino, poor, old or young—and all of those oppressions are connected. We are very focused on dismantling systems or institutions that are harmful to the flourishing of future leaders and the amazing work that can happen in our community. I'm very proud of the work we do, mostly because it ties so many of my identities together into one focus, and it allows me to spend my energy on something I care deeply about: creating a better community for everyone and making sure nobody is left behind.

When people think of philanthropy, they typically think of a white, upper-class man or woman. And then they meet me. Throw me into a philanthropy meeting, and you won't see a lot of others who look like me. I bring a very different point of view. And that's exciting.

* * * * * * * *

QUICK FACTS

♦ From four national and two state-level population surveys, it was estimated that as of 2011, approximately 9 million, or around 3.5% of the U.S. population, identify as LGBT.[1]

♦ 58% of LGBT workers reported that a coworker makes a joke or derogatory comment about LGBT people "at least once in a while."[2]

♦ 67% of LGBT employees do not report anti-LGBT remarks to human resources or management.[3]

♦ In 2010, 46% of Fortune 500 companies had nondiscrimination policies that included gender identity or gender expression, compared to 69% of the Fortune 100.[4]

- 87% of Fortune 500 companies have non-discrimination policies based on sexual orientation; 94% of Fortune 100 companies have non-discrimination policies that include sexual orientation.[5]

- In 2011, 52% of all employers offered domestic partner health insurance benefits—up from 31% in 2010.[6]

* * * * * * * *

BERNELL HOOKER

It's 1976. I'm playing in my first high school varsity basketball game. In fact, it is the first time I have ever played organized sports. So coach puts me in. I'm playing the center position. She instructs me of my role. Two minutes later...I'm sitting on the bench. I fouled out. Yes, fouled out in TWO MINUTES.

I quickly learned the game in high school. I also learned how to play volleyball and became an all-city shot put and discus thrower. My letter sweater had tri-athlete, numerous varsity letters and chevrons and a front load of medals. I took to sports like a fish takes to water. I received a scholarship for basketball to a Division II school. Can you believe that? The girl who fouled out of a game after playing two minutes.

Sports have been good to me. I'm the person I am today because of them. My resilience to move forward when the world said no has paid off.

You see, I didn't have female sports role models growing up because I didn't see such strong, empowering, and influential women on television, let alone read about them in the daily newspaper or see them in my community.

Playing Through the Fence

You've heard the phrase, if I knew then what I know now...

It was 1972 when President Richard Nixon signed Title IX of the Educational Amendment of 1972, stating that "no person in the United States shall, on the basis of sex, be excluded from participation in, be denied the benefits of, or be subjected to discrimination under any educational program or activity receiving Federal assistance."

I entered high school in 1974. I had no idea what Title IX was growing up, but I know now. I know how important it is for young girls to understand the HERSTORY of women's sports and pioneering women who have given us the freedom to play—but most importantly, to teach girls about the business of sports to open up career choices that don't welcome women.

My passion for sports stems from my late father. All through high school and college, I played sports. I took on my first college basketball coaching position in 1990. I was the only African-American woman coaching in the Division III level. In fact, there weren't any African-American women coaching in Wisconsin.

My father's words of "make it happen" were from a conversation we had before he died of cancer in 2003. The conversation centered on why young girls and parents didn't understand sports recruiting, nor did they have the skill level to play college ball. We also discussed why images of female athletes were absent in the media and on sportswear, such as t-shirts, unlike male images seen during the NCAA Basketball Championships and the Final Four.

He reminded me how he and my mother knew nothing about recruiting or college. They were blue-collar workers from Mississippi who never went to college but who stressed education to my brothers and me. I'm proud to say we all have college degrees.

I took my father's words, along with the support of my mother, to "make it happen" through IOU Sports, a nonprofit organization for girls and women that instills education

---

through sports. Growing up during the start of Title IX, I saw the importance of sports for girls and what it had done for me. I wanted to continue the HERSTORY of women's sports and pass it on to the next generation of female athletes.

The struggles girls experienced to achieve their dreams through education and sports were all too real. There weren't many organizations that focused primarily on girls, sports and leadership. When IOU Sports came on the scene in 2003, its goal was to give girls the tools they needed through scholarships, internships and employment opportunities. Providing skills in leadership development in their sport was also very important. To help accomplish this, professional female athletes were brought in to talk to them about the importance of following their dreams. Those goals continue to be practiced to this day. The leadership skills I obtained by not giving in, and not giving up, manifested through my effectiveness and dedication in IOU Sports.

It has not been easy. As I am an African-American woman, founder and CEO of this organization, the community thought it was only for African Americans. Corporations denied funding because we had sports in our mission and they were confused that it wasn't an urban program or because we weren't one of the big box organizations; therefore, we couldn't deliver programs. However, corporations and the big box organizations are now calling us requesting that we send them our grant forms or are asking to collaborate with our programs.

I have taken my passion, and the many no's I've received, to show the world that interested girls of all ethnicities who aspire to do so should have the opportunity to attain leadership skills, violence prevention training and development through various sports and sport career exploration. IOU Sports has opened the eyes of girls and their parents to the possibilities and opportunities that our foremothers have given us. Women can have a career in sports...it's a business.

Playing Through the Fence

The women of the Title IX era are now role models and have all grown up to become coaches, athletic directors, lawyers, engineers, scientists, journalists, authors, CEOs, professional athletes, aunts, mothers and grandmothers. We must continue to understand the importance of Title IX and fight for its existence. We must lead the way for the future of girls through SPORTS and the careers derived from it.

Through IOU Sports, activities and materials focus specifically on empowering girls and women through education and sports. We have increased the likelihood that girls' specific challenges and strengths will continue to be addressed in our community. At IOU Sports, we believe that improving the life options of girls will have a positive effect on their lives. We have reached thousands of girls and have had an impact not just on our local community but nationally as well.

Every girl who has been through our program has benefited from playing with other girls in a safe environment. We give them the opportunity to do something they love—improve on the sports they play and/or explore those they haven't—and meet influential female pro athletes and women who work in the NFL, NBA and MBL. Experiences like these, and the impact they have on the girls, can't be measured—but the results continue to be astounding for the 80% of the girls we follow afterward (the other 20% come from detention centers in which we have no contact with once they leave our program). The girls who were with us from the beginning are now college graduates, working in some type of sports program and/or working with youth.

We know sports make a difference in the lives of girls. As adults we lead active lifestyles. Our participation in sports and fitness insures good health and it gives us a business advantage. Why not let girls in on it at an early age?

I've never given up on my dream. I didn't allow adversity to stop me when I saw how IOU Sports helped girls—those same girls who society believed wouldn't succeed. It kept them in school, grades were better, and they were getting scholarships...I thank the men and women I connected with on my journey and those who have given me a chance and opportunity. The more that women are in positions of decision making and hiring, the more women you'll see in leadership roles.

People continue to ask if I'm still running "that program." I have to correct them and say I'm running an organization that is founded by a girl and a dream and the legacy of her father's motto, "Making it Happen." I enjoy speaking to youth and letting them know I'm from the same city in which they live. I went to public schools. I was good in sports because I didn't give up. Same with business.

As women, we have to create our own opportunities and destiny. That's what I did. The no's I received, I turned into yes's through my perseverance. My job is to teach girls that sports are a business and there's a place in it for everyone. No more old boy's network. I make it a conscious effort to give young women their start in the sports industry. I've become that decision-making executive. You see, sports have given me courage, leadership skills and the ability to work with people. I took what I've learned and empowered myself as a person who created her own destiny.

I've been empowered to show and teach other women that sports is a business, especially those who are transitioning as elite athletes trying to find their place in the corporate or entrepreneurial worlds.

My life has gone full circle. I love what I do. I'm now considered an expert. Wow, just to think that fouling out of the game in two minutes would lead me into a lifetime in the game.

"No matter what accomplishments you make,
somebody helped you."
—Tennis great, Althea Gibson

* * * * * * * *

MARY

The fastest growing segment of diversity in today's workplace comes from workers with disabilities. In my role of community involvement, I often attend events for causes my corporation supports. Recently, I was enlightened by attending an event for Milwaukee workers with disabilities, with the shared goal of creating accessible environments for workers—individuals who had high capabilities to contribute yet scarce opportunity to utilize their skills.

The guest speaker was Amy Roloff, star of the popular cable show, *Little People. Big World.* I had never seen her show; however, several guests at my table had been inspired by her story. Her speech was riveting, and her message was poignant: People with disabilities are highly capable, have an extreme desire to contribute, and are often overlooked for what they don't have, regardless of what they can contribute.

* * * * * * * *

BECKY TROCHINSKI

I was born in 1971 with Juvenile Muscular Dystrophy and Juvenile Spinal Muscular Atrophy. My brother also had MD. He died when he was three and I was two. My parents, especially my father, had a hard time with our disabilities, but they dealt with them in very different ways. My father couldn't accept that both his kids had a disability. After my brother's death, my parents' marriage fell apart under the strain. They divorced when I was six.

A Moment to Decide—Choosing to Persevere

My mother was the only family member who could handle caring for me. When I look back at old home movies, I see the sadness in her face. She sacrificed so much for me: her body, her plans and her dreams. Mom didn't work until after the divorce. Later, she remarried and relocated us to Minnesota, where we lived in a 100-year-old farmhouse, which was very difficult for me to maneuver. We had a St. Bernard, Ben, who would let me grab onto his fur and help me around. My first real attachment was to that dog.

Later, others were willing to help me. My school bus driver would sling me over his shoulder to get me on the bus (at that time, there were no special accommodations or buses for disabled students) and, because the school was two stories, students and teachers would carry me up and down the stairs. At first I was horrified to be spotlighted like that, but I soon realized that other people besides my mom were willing to help, and that was a blessing.

When I grew too big to be carried, I was put into a wheelchair, which upset me. I knew once I sat in a wheelchair, I probably would never get out. By the age of 12, I was dependent on a wheelchair every day and could no longer make it up the stairs of our home, meaning I had to sleep in the living room and use a portable toilet. We'd sectioned off a makeshift bathroom with a green curtain, but it was still embarrassing when friends came over.

Eventually, my mom divorced again and we moved to Hartford, Wisconsin, where we had family. My cousins became very important to me. They didn't let me miss anything—going to parks and parties, getting into trouble. They never let my disability stop us. I became a great excuse for being late to class, and people loved to pile onto my wheelchair and roll down hills.

But still there were times when it was apparent I was different. People would stare at me, and parents would shush their kids to stop them from asking questions. I would rather have had the questions than the shush, so I would often stick my tongue out at them so they would have something to look at. People would call me a "faker" because I could still move my legs. And my high-school guidance counselor told me I should be a secretary so I could just sit behind a desk all day. That really agitated me, and I said to myself, "No way. I am going to show you."

Eventually, the Lions Club provided me with an electric wheelchair. It was the first time someone else didn't need to push me; that was very liberating. I lived a mile from school, and before, my friends had to push me—but after I got the electric chair, I would travel on the road (the town didn't have curb ramps). Once the police stopped me, since I technically wasn't supposed to be on the street. I wrote an article, and because of the response, curb ramps were installed. I also complained about the post office since it wasn't wheelchair accessible. I learned that you need to speak up and advocate to change things.

I joined Students For an Accessible Society (SFAS), which taught me to speak up and not be ashamed of my disability. You can't complain about something if you're not willing to fix it. Through SFAS, I've spoken to clubs and college classes to bring awareness about life in a wheelchair. I'll answer any question—even about sex. (In case you're wondering, here's the answer: I do everything that you do; I just do it differently, and it may take me longer.)

College was difficult for me. Living in the dorms was one of the worst experiences of my life because I had to ask new people for help—and sometimes it never came. I struggled with attendant care. SFAS taught me to stand up for myself and ask for help, although it was difficult. It gave me a sense of community, like my own little sorority, which I called the Tri Gimps—Gimpa Gimpa Gimpa. (You have to have a sense of humor!) When I graduated, my advisor said he didn't think anyone would ever hire me. Again, I thought, I'll show you.

Being an art teacher comes with a lot of physical requirements, but I never missed a day in student teaching. When I completed my student teaching, the dean of my college gave me a hug. It was one of the biggest accomplishments of my life. Now to find a job!

I applied at 100 school districts in 20 states and only got a one-semester art teacher job in a Wisconsin middle school. Because she knew my professional life would be a struggle and I couldn't find adequate attendant care, my mother moved to the apartment next to me. She came over every day at 4 AM to help me get ready for work. Although I had to leave an hour and a half early to get to work on time, I never missed a day. Rolling down the hallway to my classroom made me so proud.

I received a Master's degree while I was working full-time, and I'm now a teacher at a technology high school. I've won two personal achievement awards from the MD Association. When I received my last award, I said it should have gone to my mom. How could I ever repay her for everything she's done for me? She's still one of the biggest reasons I'm successful today.

Another reason: the man of my dreams, whom I've been with for the past 10 years. We have two children together but haven't married, because a legal marriage would mean I would lose my benefits to help with attendant care. I believe we are married in God's eyes.

I was amazed when we got pregnant. When I was 13, doctors told me I probably wouldn't want to have children because they would turn out like me. My parents and many friends were frightened that the pregnancy was going to be too much for my body and I wouldn't be able to find help for my newborn. The pregnancy was great, but the birthing process was difficult. I had to be put under for my C-section, and I had a hard time getting off the ventilator in Intensive Care. I had to fight hard to see my daughter, who was the most incredible accomplishment of my life. She was so beautiful it took my breath away.

Three days after I got home from the hospital, I fell while an attendant was helping me into the shower, and I broke my pelvis. The break wasn't discovered until months later, and two years later, when I was pregnant with my son, my pelvic bones separated from the birthing process. Because of my MD, my pelvis will never heal properly. I'm now living with a tremendous amount of pain. I try to express my frustrations with my body through my art and through focusing on my beautiful children.

I think about what my life would be like if I hadn't gone on to school or become a teacher. I would not have my house, or two beautiful kids, or a man who loves me. None of that would have happened if I had sat home and felt sorry for myself over my disability. You have to believe in yourself and keep trying.

While my life hasn't been easy, I've never been willing to listen to those who said I couldn't accomplish whatever I set my mind to. Life is hard work, but there are so many great things that come along with working hard. I sometimes forget to look back at what I've accomplished, but when I do, I am proud of what I've done. I had a choice: to believe the people who said I'd never go to college, get a job or have children, or to live my dreams. I chose to live.

* * * * * * * *

QUICK FACTS

♦ Just over 1 in 4 of today's 20 year-olds will become disabled before they retire.[7]

♦ Over 37 million Americans are classified as disabled; about 12% of the total population. More than 50% of those disabled Americans are in their working years, from 18-64.[8]

♦ 8.8 million disabled wage earners, over 5% of U.S. workers were receiving Social Security Disability (SSDI) benefits at the end of 2012.[9]

A Moment to Decide—Choosing to Persevere

MARY

Many of us, myself included, believe that obstacles are synonymous with crisis. The word "crisis" is Greek, meaning "a moment to decide." These moments of crisis and decisions are opportunities to choose a path and move from one place to another. We grow both from the good decisions we make and the bad ones. The bigger the challenge and obstacle, the bigger potential for growth.

We, as human beings, and especially as women, need to embrace challenges and obstacles as opportunities to grow. There is no easy path or how-to workshop on overcoming these obstacles. But the one thing a person cannot do when faced with an obstacle is to do nothing. Obstacles and challenges in our lives and careers are numerous and temporary. The only obstacles that are permanent are the ones you decide not to challenge.

If you select a group of people and give them the same challenge, it is likely that each member of the group will chose a different tactic or strategy to overcome the challenge. Each person may take a different approach, and each one may become successful at it. Here are a few guidelines for success:

- Keep at it. Continue putting one foot in front of the other.
- Be mindful of what is working as you chip away at the challenge. Keep doing it.
- Be mindful of what is not working as you chip away at the challenge. Tweak it. Try something new.
- Find someone who has achieved what you seek to achieve. Talk to them and/or research how they did it and how it applies to your situation. Adjust. Adapt.
- Acknowledge the process of learning and growing. Use perspective and success of past challenges you have overcome to find the inner faith that you can do it again.

EXERCISE

What obstacles are you facing in your personal or professional life that you believe are keeping you from achieving your goals?

....

....

....

....

....

....

....

What have you done to try to overcome these obstacles?

....

....

....

....

....

....

....

A Moment to Decide—Choosing to Persevere

What is working well, and what is not?

....

....

....

....

....

Who do you know (personally or through other means) who has had the same obstacle(s) and was successful overcoming it?

....

....

....

....

....

....

What are the lessons that you can take away from their experience, or if you do not know, how could you reach out to them to find out?

....

....

....

....

....

NOTES

....

....

....

....

....

....

....

....

....

....

....

....

....

....

....

....

....

....

Chapter Two
It Takes a Village
Family Support

"Call it a clan, call it a network, call it a tribe, call it a family.
Whatever you call it, whoever you are, you need one."
— Jane Howard, Author

MARY

What does family have to do with professional success? In my own experience and for many of the successful women I've encountered, the answer is a lot. Family is the backbone that provides the confidence and support you need to reach for your dreams—and it's the net that catches you when you fall trying.

To me, families are much like mentorships that start at birth. Family relationships provide the crucial guidance and foundation needed to successfully help one grow and develop personally as well as professionally. Key business skills such as teamwork, conflict resolution and communication are learned at home.

My salt-of-the-earth parents instilled strong, sound values of right and wrong in my five siblings and me. Both my parents worked hard, and worked together, to ensure that their children had the best they could offer to us. They taught us to respect each other and, above all, to love each other. My mother would often say, "You're all each other has; it's important you know that and respect it."

My family was, and still is, a tight-knit group. In some ways this closeness was our choice, and in other ways it was due to circumstance—such as all eight of us having to spend many years sharing one bathroom. The boys weren't so bad, but having three sisters to compete with meant I had to learn diplomacy quickly and at an early age. After I married, my dream was to have daughters of my own, and I am blessed with two. When they were young, I told them the same thing my mother had said to us: "You are all each other has. Love and respect each other." My husband and I have made an effort to prepare our daughters for the workplace, let them know they can achieve whatever they want in life and that they can accomplish as much as anyone else, male or female.

We instilled basic expectations for our girls—such as being on time for appointments, maintaining good eye contact during conversations, and dressing appropriately for occasions. My husband always added, "Give them a firm handshake." Both of our daughters have always known that an education is essential, especially for women, as we wanted them to be as self-reliant as possible. We taught them the importance of going the extra mile, setting yourself apart from the pack and delivering on promises.

Times are different now than they were decades ago. Many households today are managed by only one parent. Many women now assume the working role, while their husbands stay home to take care of the house and children. Since the economic downturn, jobs are not as prevalent as they were in the past. Therefore, the need for support from extended family members and others (a network of friends, mentors, neighbors, etc.) is more important than ever before.

There is a growing need to help children who lack the support of two nurturing parents. There is a need for school systems to improve graduation rates. There is a need for our community to figure out a strategy to significantly combat and decrease the escalating teen pregnancy rate. Aunts, uncles, cousins, and some-times even neighbors have had to step up to fill the obvious void so prevalent in many households today to ensure the well-being of our next generation of leaders for our communities.

* * * * * * * *

MARIA MONREAL-CAMERON

In the 1920s, my parents and maternal grandmother, all Mexican immigrants, settled in Texas, where seven of my older siblings were born.

My dad had a good job with the railroad. My mother, along with my older siblings, harvested vegetables near our homestead in Ennis, Texas. Life was good but difficult, and after hearing of increased opportunities North, my mother persuaded my dad to make the hard trek to Milwaukee, Wisconsin.

My parents, grandmother and siblings arrived in Milwaukee in the early 1940s, and Wisconsin became the birthplace of the remaining six Monreal children, myself included. I am one of 13 children born to Mexican immigrant parents and the first female after seven males.

My parents did not find a large Mexican community in Milwaukee, but the small community that did exist was a close-knit one. The early immigrants formed social organizations that adhered to cultural customs and traditions and also provided a social and professional network.

During my early childhood, I recall having Serbian, Polish and Greek neighbors. These distinct ethnicities seemed to share the near south side remarkably well. Although our language and traditions were very different, it was an era of good neighbor practices. During those early years, I also recall a handful of Hispanic-owned businesses.

Although my first language was Spanish, once I was enrolled in school, I was expected to excel in all English, government and history classes. As a result of this, I am fiercely proud of my Mexican heritage as well as my American birthright.

To many, the bare biological facts may sound harsh...a large family, a language barrier, financial constraints. The reality is that my upbringing occurred in a humble but emotionally rich environment. My nurturing parents and loving maternal grandmother instilled in each and every one of us a strong work ethic, a never-quit attitude and strong moral and religious convictions.

Admittedly, I have encountered prejudice and bias based not only on my ethnicity but also my gender. Unfortunately, the most disconcerting has been dealing with my own ethnicity's "macho" mentality.

For many years, Latina women have been simply identified as mothers, sisters and wives. Our society has done very little to encourage Latina women to think beyond those narrowly defined and horribly confining roles that seem to be handed down from generation to generation. It is only within the last two decades that we have begun to realize and experience a small portion of our full potential. More importantly, we are becoming aware that we do not have to accept the roles dictated to us by society, but that we can, in fact, take control of our own lives and determine our own destinies.

We must freely share a new vision for Latina upward mobility. We must dare to release the culturally embedded norms, so prevalent in Hispanic communities, which prevent Latinas from realizing their full potential.

The best way to predict the future is to create it. While the future is not entirely up to us, there is much we can do to shape its outcome. We must continue to be intolerant of mediocrity. We must attain, through our own merits, positions of influence and authority.

I believe that success has nothing to do with luck. Success is earned and should not be viewed as an entitlement. My professional success is based on fundamental principles of determination, discipline and dedication. It is important for Latina leaders to leave footprints for other Latinas to follow.

My journey has not been easy, but it has been unbelievably rewarding. My stresses, demands and workload are extraordinarily intense. I manage a very hectic career and make sacrifices to accommodate my responsibilities as a wife, mother and professional, while trying to do everything to the nth degree. I live life to its fullest and try to smile in spite of difficult times.

I am grateful to have been given the opportunity to work for my Hispanic community. I have never forgotten that I am the daughter of Mexican vegetable pickers, that I am a woman whose father held jobs as a railroad and foundry worker, whose mother worked as a dishwasher and tannery worker, or whose parents never finished grade school.

I proudly serve as president and CEO of a widely regarded and respected, award-winning Hispanic Chamber of Commerce for my state. I have even been bestowed with an honorary doctorate degree for my work. Despite obstacles and challenges, this Mexican-American has experienced and continues to live The American Dream.

* * * * * * * *

Playing Through the Fence

* * * * * * * *

DEBRA CRAWFORD

In April 2009, my sister, brother and I went to surprise my father for his 75th birthday. My brother helped us contact two of Dad's oldest friends, who came over for lunch. It had been more than three decades since we had witnessed this kind of gathering of our elders. Growing up, my siblings and I would often find our living room full of wonderful, strong black men and women discussing how to overcome the challenges they faced because of our race. They were my first introduction to change agents and leaders.

And now, here they sat—three 75-year-old black men, entrepreneurs who also raised families, taught moral values and led by example, all gathered to celebrate friendship and endurance while recalling civil rights activism.

The men settled in and began to talk. My dad recalled a memory of traveling to worksites as a glazier with white counterparts to install glass. At lunchtime, they disappeared while my father ate in the truck. One day he decided to follow them, only to discover that they were in the restaurant enjoying a meal while he ate alone. Because of the color of his skin, he couldn't enter the restaurant with them. Dad began to drive himself to the sites.

While my dad undoubtedly walked the talk, so did my mother. She insisted that we learn etiquette and that we were well mannered, disciplined and educated. She wouldn't tolerate weakness. She insisted that we walk into difficult situations with pride and without showing fear, no matter how we felt inside. It was the strength and determination I learned through them that helped me when a man on the street decided to spit in my hair. It helped me when my seventh grade Irish classmates, who often came to my house, informed me that I couldn't enter their homes but could remain in the driveway.

It took a lot of years of experience with racial issues before I developed the confidence to exercise my own personal power and choices, reject those kinds of friendships and not subject myself to little-minded people.

After college, I moved to Chicago for my first management position with a Fortune 500 retailer. When looking for an apartment, my co-workers kindly directed me to those neighborhoods where I would be welcome and away from those I'd better avoid. Unfortunately, I still had the humbling experience of stumbling on a landlord who connected well with me over the phone, only to refuse to let me in when she looked out of her window to discover a black woman.

Perplexed, I promptly went to a pay phone, and we enjoyed a pleasant reconnection. She asked when I was coming and was shocked when I explained that I was the woman who had just knocked on her door. She stammered, and then offered to let me fill out the application—on the back stairs. She said her husband wouldn't allow her to let blacks in their apartment.

The strength and determination that I learned from my family also helped in my career, when I was often the only black manager, director or vice-president. During the Affirmative Action movement, many young black professionals were firsts. We were being sent to unfamiliar locations across the country without the benefit of family, friends, a support system or many people who looked like us. We were sent to locations that were sometimes unwelcoming of young, ambitious, educated black men and women.

We had to press ahead anyway. A lot of people had struggled and died to help open doors for us to go through. People back home were proud of our accomplishments and we had to "represent." We had to have courage, to get up when we made mistakes, to learn new rules of engagement, and to operate without being mentored on corporate expectations. Often we were the first generationally, so we couldn't phone home to ask about strategy—but we could always phone home to be encouraged to be strong, work hard, and never settle for less than what we were capable of.

I didn't always feel like a soldier like my parents; but from them, I knew success was the best revenge against those who would have liked to hold me down. When I began to work in corporate situations, I sometimes feared the unfamiliar, but I always walked confidently onto airplanes and into hotels, restaurants, department stores and organizations.

I didn't get upset when, during an interview, I was asked if I felt like I was a token. I said no. My interviewer and others may have felt that way, but I didn't. I said I wasn't looking for a handout; I just wanted them to open the door and get out of my way. I never chose to let those who felt uncomfortable about my presence stand in my way.

When I graduated from college, my dad said, "People have fought so that you have tremendous opportunities. Know that the world is your oyster; go and find your pearl."

Listening to my dad and his friends recall where we have been as a people and brag about the accomplishments of their adult children, I am reminded of how far we have come—and how far we still have to go. The men are cynical, to some degree, about how much ground we still have to cover. But they are so proud of our president, a black man. They shake their heads as they consider just how far things have come in their lifetime. And as for me, well, I pray my grandchildren can go and "find their pearls" without experiencing the barriers of old.

* * * * * * * *

It Takes a Village—Family Support

MARY

Hillary Rodham Clinton famously declared, "It takes a village..." Although she used this phrase in the context of the challenges of raising children and creating a network of family and support around oneself to help raise them to be happy, healthy people, I also think this concept extends to all of us in life.

No man or woman is an island. We are who we are because of the people we surround ourselves with. Another quip I love is "Show me your friends, and I'll show you your future." I have found this to be true.

In a 2013 study of 250+ entrepreneurs who had founded small- to medium-sized businesses, the following support systems were positively related to success and satisfaction for female business owners:[1]

- **Affective Family-to-Business Enrichment:** The transfer of positive affect, or mood/happiness, from the family domain to the work domain;

- **Instrumental Family-to-Business Enrichment:** The transfer of skills/behaviors acquired or nurtured in the family domain to the work domain;

- **Family-to-Business Support:** Interpersonal support from family members.

These systems were not related to entrepreneurial success for male business owners, for which researchers suggest two explanations: 1) Female entrepreneurs may benefit from family support more than men due to their relative lack of access to other resources such as social and financial capital; and 2) Women's tendency to integrate work and family as well as to place emphasis on relationships in general may give them an advantage in capitalizing on family enrichment and support.

Support networks are vital to personal growth. The role of a support network is to keep you motivated, hold you accountable and encourage you. They provide words of wisdom and constructive criticism at the right time. They are with you through your journey of life and help you navigate critical paths in your career.

Chapter Three

Fighting the Battle

Nature vs. Nurture

"Women are the largest untapped reservoir of talent in the world."
— Hillary Rodham Clinton, Former First Lady of the United States, Former US Secretary of State

MARY

Our gender is determined by genetics, while our sex is programmed by social customs. Each individual has pressure placed upon them based on their gender, and many continue to hang onto old-fashioned notions of a woman's place versus a man's. However, the economy has created a role reversal in many families today. There is an increasing number of men who now assume the role of Mr. Mom, while their wives are the primary wage earners for the family. I'll never forget Hillary Rodham Clinton's famous declaration, "I suppose I could have stayed home and baked cookies and had teas, but what I decided to do was to fulfill my profession which I entered before my husband was in public life."

Now more than ever, women hold jobs that have been traditionally male dominated. In 2012, women made up 46.9% of the workforce[1] and comprised 51.5% of management, professional and related positions.[2] However, the news isn't all good. Even though progress has been made, it's being made slowly. In many industries, there is little change in women securing jobs traditionally held by men. There are still too few women in the top jobs—in fact, out of 45 countries examined, the United States ranks in the bottom ten for the percentage of women in senior management positions (22%).[3]

Four out of ten women work in traditionally female occupations, while 43.7% of men work in traditionally male occupations—and yet women are still earning less than men in each of the most common occupations for women.[4]

Is gender equality still out of reach? I feel confident that in time we will chip away at the assumption that men and women are happier when fulfilling the roles nature determined for them. Nature is changing because of nurture, and therefore, so will our roles. We are raising new generations of women who are told they can do more, be more, and achieve more—and therefore, they will.

FIVE LEADING OCCUPATIONS FOR EMPLOYED WOMEN (2010)

1. Secretaries and administrative assistants
2. Registered nurses
3. Elementary and middle school teachers
4. Cashiers
5. Retail salespersons

(*Source: Department of Labor*)

Fighting the Battle—Nature vs. Nurture

* * * * * * * *

DELORIS SIMS

Bittersweet...Almost 30 years ago, I started as a part-time teller at a bank, in the same building that later housed the bank I would co-own with two other minority women. It still amazes me that within this same building where it took me years to even get a full-time job, I later became chairman and CEO.

When I started working at the bank, I didn't have a college degree. But I related to the bank's customers, who were most often African American like me and weren't educated about banking. I knew I could teach them. I also helped them secure business loans, which had been previously problematic. Our operations turned around, and we became profitable. The bank was even awarded for customer service.

Customers and co-workers praised me for my leadership skills. But when a promotion became available, it was given to one of my co-workers, who was less qualified—but white. My managers told me that the area wasn't ready for a minority manager.

Eventually, however, I became the operations manager and later became a branch manager—a surprising promotion for which I was unprepared. In order to learn about business loans, I sent myself back to school. I was passionate about community economic development and helping minorities get ahead in the system, and I also had a desire to learn and to succeed in my own career.

Soon after I was named branch manager, my bosses asked me to fire one of our black employees—a man. I refused and said I would train him. I said that together, we would go over bad loans and ask ourselves how we could do it differently—and we did. We learned a lot together, and he eventually became a vice president at the bank. Taking that extra step isn't the norm, but it's how I gained the respect of my co-workers for 28 years.

But it wasn't always easy; my peers were white men who weren't happy about having me, an African-American woman, as an equal team member. Some of them would do anything to break me, including making derogatory comments about black people. One man told me he liked living up north because of the "white sand." I later found out that he was referring to the primarily white population. It was hard working with people who were trying to sabotage me, and who didn't like me, but I never backed down. I was going to out-perform them every chance I could.

When I was promoted to vice president and business banker, I changed locations. A prejudiced manager once told me that customers didn't want to deal with blacks or women. So I sent a memo to the head of personnel. I knew I was dealing with one individual's racism and not a bank policy, and I had to challenge that.

I have always been very self-confident, a trait which I attribute to my mother, growing up in a family of 10 children, and to The Man Upstairs. I ask God for wisdom in every aspect of my life—from making risky career moves (like giving loans to people who wanted to buy houses in the neighborhood, although I was told not to) to raising my two children, who sometimes had to come to work with me.

I've also found and affiliated myself with support groups. I was in charge of business banking for a group that helps minority bankers get promoted. I worked in the centralized lending department with two men, and we had one of the most profitable, diverse customer bases. I am also a member of my state's African American Women Ltd. Our goal is to leave something behind to help other businesswomen. Through the group, I met my partners in the bank.

Fighting the Battle—Nature vs. Nurture

Starting the bank was one of the greatest risks of my life. Like my partners, I invested $150,000 of my own money, and together we raised almost $7 million for the bank—mostly from locals who, like us, were outraged by the way area banks had been treating minorities. (A 1988 survey by the U.S. Department of Housing showed that 24 percent of black mortgage applicants in my area were turned down for loans, versus just 6 percent of white loan applicants.)

One investor, an attorney and former CEO of a Major League Baseball team, decided to help us because he thought the idea of three black women owning a bank in the inner city was "sexy." Regardless of their reasons, people stepped up and, after 18 months, we were able to open the bank.

At the age of 65, I owned one of the fastest growing banks in the country. When we opened in 1999 we had $7 million in assets, and we grew to $235 million. Our goal was to grow to $400 million in assets, but our main goal was to rebuild this area, our neighborhood.

We started a redevelopment corporation and partnered with the Housing Authority to build 11 blocks of homes and refurbish area buildings. We taught entrepreneurship through a joint venture with a literacy program. At an awards dinner, we raised $200,000 to be given as grants to deserving organizations. We also partnered with a foundation providing educational support for under-resourced communities for 15 years, providing the group $50,000 in operating expenses each year. And we helped our customers by giving them very personalized service and advice for running their businesses. We wanted to make a difference.

Not too long ago, my sister was diagnosed with terminal cancer; she was gone in six months. It taught me to please myself, not others, and to be true to myself. It's something I will continue to do for my career, my community, and myself.

QUICK FACTS

THE GOOD:

♦ As of 2012, there were 911,728 African-American women-owned businesses (non-farm) in the U.S, representing a 191.4% increase since 1997 and a 66.7% increase since 2002.[5]

THE BAD:

♦ As of 2013, women in the United States are paid 77 cents for every dollar paid to men on average. This disparity is worse for African-American women, who are earning 70 cents for every dollar paid to men and just 64 cents for every dollar paid to white men.[6]

* * * * * * * *

JOAN KESSLER

I spent my early years, while my father was a soldier in WWII, with my mother and maternal grandparents in the Texas panhandle. The only person of color with whom I had any contact that I remember was the woman who worked for my grandmother as a domestic. I adored both my grandmother and this wonderful woman who played with me, gave me treats, and seemed to think I was wonderful. I remember her as sort of mysterious because she was very dark and very kind. After we moved away from Texas, we still came back for summers and Christmas holidays. Until I was about eight, she still worked for my grandmother, and I still adored them both. I did not understand why she didn't eat with us when she had fixed the meal; when I asked, my mother or grandmother changed the subject.

Fighting the Battle—Nature vs. Nurture

When the war ended, my parents and I moved to a small town near Dallas, where my father was working. I have no memory of seeing anyone of color anywhere in that town. When I was about four, history repeated itself when we moved to Kansas City. Everyone with whom I remember having any contact was as white as me. When I went to grade school and high school, there were no people of color in any class I ever had; our "diversity" was a small number of Jewish kids. It was like living in a large bowl of white rice— everyone was the same. And it was bland. But at the same time, my mother kept telling me that I was smart enough that I could be anything I wanted to be if I worked hard enough. Not only did I actually believe her (I hadn't yet figured out that being female had certain economic disadvantages at that time), but she gave me the distinct impression that the premise applied to everyone.

I went to college full of confidence and expectations. The University of Kansas (KU) was the only school where I could put together enough financial aid so I could afford to go. Through the school's programs and scholarships, I had managed to live in Paris one summer and near Munich another summer. Particularly the experience in France made it clear to me that the world was much more colorful and interesting than the places I'd lived. I needed to find a place where everyone did not look or think pretty much the same.

I had no one I was interested in marrying, and I certainly did not want to spend my life studying or teaching French and/or German. This no doubt influenced my radical (for the time) conclusion to go to law school. My mother was generally supportive; my grandfather could not understand why I didn't just get a good job as a secretary. Nonetheless, my grandfather helped me a bit financially, and I was off to lay the groundwork for a career that almost no women pursued at that time (early 1960s).

The University of Wisconsin was the best law school to which I was accepted *and* for which I was able to cobble together enough by way of scholarships and cash to pay the costs of my education. I arrived at law school completely unprepared for how hard the work would be compared to my college experience. I was also unprepared for how few women there were in law school. I remember less than six other women law students in a student body of about nine hundred.

So began my first inkling of what it might be like to be in a visible social minority. I quickly learned that being constantly surrounded by so many men, in the most competitive environment I had ever experienced, had both negative and positive aspects. The biggest positive was the plentiful offers of dates. I later married and transferred to Marquette University Law School in Milwaukee, where I finished in 1968. When I began as a lawyer in Milwaukee, I could count on the fingers of one hand the number of other women lawyers practicing there. It was a lonely place professionally. I had to convince judges and court personnel that I was not a messenger. I had to convince my male colleagues' (that's redundant, actually) wives that I was not a threat to them. I had to convince my male opponents in court that I was competent, reasonable and trustworthy. And I had to do this while being a mom, a politician's wife, and determined to do what I could to make our city and state a better place for people of all colors to live. That plate was pretty full.

As a result of years of active participation, when Jimmy Carter was elected President, I was selected as the United States Attorney for the eastern half of the state of Wisconsin. There had never been a woman in that office before. I was 35 and an active member of the ACLU. I was the chief law enforcement officer for the federal government in that geographic area. I had to work with the Special Agent in Charge of the local office of the FBI; without his office, I couldn't prosecute many crimes, and without my office, his investigations couldn't be charged as crimes. He was in his late fifties, had been in law enforcement all his adult life, and was clearly not comfortable with me. I had a few misgivings myself. We learned to get past our respective stereotypes and work out differences so that we could both be effective in our jobs. I also learned how differently (deferentially) I was treated as a person with power, compared to the way I was treated by many people before I had the power of that job.

Today, I find myself looking back to try to understand why I am here and what I am to do with what I have learned. I want to leave a better world for my grandchildren. I still struggle with how much race relations have changed and how much they remain the same. The Civil Rights Act of 1964 and the Voting Rights Act of 1965 were enormously important progress. Nonetheless, we still face huge problems that we cannot afford not to solve. Systemic public policies have had unintentional but visible and devastating impacts on our country. White privilege remains a concept so ingrained in our social fabric that it is not recognized at all by many who benefit from it. Perhaps acknowledging the problems, and talking about them, is the first and most important step to solving them.

* * * * * * * *

SHANON VUCKOVIC

Spending part of my childhood growing up on a reservation in Wisconsin, I did not necessarily look like the other Native American children I attended school with. Although my skin tone and eye color were true to my heritage, my blonde hair indicated otherwise to my classmates. Spending the remaining part of my childhood growing up in a predominately white suburb (where there too, I did not look like the other kids I attended grade school with), I was picked on for being "the Indian girl."

To this day, many people I meet in corporate America identify me as a Caucasian female when, in fact, I identify as Native American Indian. Numerous encounters about my race and/or assumptions about my ethnic background demonstrated how others viewed me based solely on the physical traits they could see. As a young woman whose mother told her she could do or be anything when she grew up, I never thought my race or gender would be a challenge; however, I learned early on that my gender, and those who shared my gender, would prove to sometimes be my biggest hurdle.

As women, I believe we are often competitive with each other. That said, I do believe competition can be good to an extent—as long as it does not tear down you or your colleagues in the process. Over the years I have personally witnessed cattiness and lack of support that women can display as a means of elevating themselves in the eyes of others. Such was the case with a woman named Sandy, for whom I worked early in my professional career.

Sandy and I got along famously the first few years I reported to her. I knew that more than anything, she wanted to be my friend. While this was okay, I had learned earlier on in my career that this created the possibility for certain challenges. Nonetheless, I forged on, created a working rapport and friendship with Sandy. I worked diligently to prove my value to her team and to not allow our friendship to influence our working relationship.

During my tenure working with and for Sandy, my role and responsibility level changed. I progressed within our organization rather quickly. I was promoted, and shortly afterward, Sandy's engagement with me changed. She suddenly seemed to have an aversion to teach and mentor me in my new position. This became quickly apparent not only to me, but to my colleagues. She began to ignore my email communications that asked for her support. When my follow-up correspondences were further ignored, I was determined to find resolve and would schedule time to speak to her "live."

Those conversations were often short, snappy and never truly resolved any of the agenda items on my ever-growing list of follow-ups for Sandy. My approach and communication with her remained professional, although I noticed I had to chase her. I noticed she often tried to schedule time with me outside of the normal workday or when I already had time scheduled to be out of the office. I learned rather quickly that these communications were a form of bullying. As a result, I began keeping everything on a high level with Sandy and was cautious to no longer share much about my personal life in order to keep our communications strictly professional.

I had witnessed words of commendation being shared with Sandy about our colleagues and the stellar customer service they provided to our businesses and client partner sites throughout the country. I saw this as a multifaceted opportunity for her to share the words of praise with not only our executive teams globally, but also with our colleagues, who should have heard those words of praise. Elevating those around me both personally and professionally is an area that has always been very near and dear to my heart. She did not share the praise with anyone.

I began to realize that Sandy was working rather strategically with what appeared to be a malicious intent to destroy my character. I noticed on many occasions how she would twist my words in such a manner that my teammates, colleagues, subordinates and even leadership began to question my character and integrity. It was a very challenging time, and I felt like I was living on a movie set. How could this be happening to me? Was I imagining it? How could my direct supervisor make strides to tarnish my character and pit my team against me? I was not and am not the type of person who thinks anyone is out to get her, but the evidence was certainly stacking up that Sandy was not a fan of mine. I knew I had to proceed carefully.

Always wanting to give Sandy the benefit of the doubt, I decided to reflect inward and started my journey there. I eventually sought out a professional mentor who was (and still is) an invaluable resource to me. She had struggled with a similar situation early on in her career and had helped me identify the root of the problem: How do I work with someone who does not have my best interest at heart?

As I reflect on my time with Sandy, I feel strongly that albeit it very challenging, this was an incredible learning opportunity. I kept reminding myself that this was only a step in the direction I wanted to go. I was not going to allow my success or my career goals to be contingent on what Sandy allowed it to be. Sandy taught me a great deal, but much of it was how *not* to treat people. To this day, I still truly believe that part of my job responsibility in supporting the person I report to is to elevate them within our organization and to ensure I am doing all I can do to help in their success. When they look good, so do I. When I succeed, so do they. I would not allow my personal integrity to be tarnished and at the end of the day my name goes wherever I go, regardless of who I work for or with. I have made a personal commitment to not allow anyone to blemish my name or character. That commitment has allowed me to focus on what is important to me: personal growth and development in my career progression.

Since the start of my professional career 20-plus years ago, I have been able to preserve numerous life lessons that helped significantly shape and truly evolve my engagements both personally and professionally. I love to hear the words "you can't" or for someone to suggest I cannot do something in my career. With obstacles or hurdles thrown in front of me, I am eager to tackle the task at hand and welcome the opportunity to prove my readiness to learn and succeed. I have found over the years that I am only as good as the people I have surrounded myself with. Letting go of personal and professional relationships that made me feel like I was drowning became easier for me as I became more confident in my ability to do the job I was hired for and exceed not only my expectations but my employers and those I support. The confidence piece was initially a challenge, but now I know I do well and I truly own that statement.

"When people show you who they are, believe them," said Maya Angelou. I reflect on this statement and hold it to be true in both my professional and my personal engagements. I want to be viewed as a hard working, ethical, motivated woman, capable of taking on any and all challenges that are presented to me. I want to be a valued resource to those I encounter and to be a trusted confidant, friend, employee and partner. When I show people who I am, I want them to believe me, trust in my abilities and know them to be true.

A close friend recently pointed out that I am a survivor, and that statement struck a chord in me. This is now another declaration that I own: "I AM A SURVIVOR." Whatever challenges I have faced in the last 20+ years, I have worked to put a positive spin on. Everything in my life, personal or professional, has become a teachable moment that I hold onto, learn from and grow from. The pearl I hold onto and continue to remind myself of to this day is that I am motivated, and if I want it bad enough, I am going to get it and achieve my goals. That 'it' could be anything. It is not that I deserve it – I have earned it. I am proud of my accomplishments and continue to strive to be successful in this and the next chapter of my career.

* * * * * * * *

QUICK FACTS

THE GOOD:

♦ As of 2013, there are an estimated 111,400 firms owned by Native American women—a 108% increase from 1997. These businesses employ 44,900 workers and contribute 28% of the revenue generated by Native American/Alaska Native-owned businesses.[7]

THE BAD:

♦ American Indian women earn just 60% of white men's earnings.[8]

♦ The poverty rates for black, Hispanic and Native American women are more than three times higher than for white non-Hispanic men. As of 2012, Native American women held the highest poverty rate of all women (34.4%).[9]

Chapter Four
Breaking the Mold
Mentors and Role Models

---

*"A mentor is someone who allows you
to see the hope inside yourself."*
— Oprah Winfrey, American Media Proprietor, Talk Show Host,
Actress, Producer, Philanthropist

MARY

Mentoring is an extremely valuable asset from both a personal and professional perspective. There are many views on the definition of mentoring, but traditionally, mentoring involves activities conducted by a person (the mentor) for another person (the mentee) in order to help that person do a job more effectively and/or to progress in his or her career.

My own definition of a mentor is someone with whom you identify (not necessarily matched with through some slick corporate initiative) and connect; who you trust, without fear, to help you develop, grow and learn. A mentor who wants you to be your best sets the stage for openness, honesty and, above all, the comfort level necessary to learn what he or she has to teach.

Your mentor should be considered a "safe haven" for you, even if he or she is tough or may challenge you from time to time, as your relationship is built on trust. You, the mentee, accept the advice that's offered based on the security of your relationship and the confidence that your mentor cares about you, your progress and your career.

I have always had mentors in my life, usually informal ones. One of my first mentors was Bob, a middle-aged white male who helped me when I started my challenging work in human resources. He was my manager at the time, and I knew when I met him during the interview that we had good chemistry. Even before he hired me, I knew he was someone I felt comfortable with and could trust. I could readily sense that he genuinely wanted me to grow, develop and be the best I could be.

After I was hired, not only could I see Bob's commitment to my development, I could feel it. As my manager and mentor, Bob never hesitated to tell me when I didn't step up to the plate or when I fell short on a project. During one of our discussions early in my career, he conveyed that he noticed I tended to be very quiet in meetings. He said he thought I had a lot to offer and that our one-on-one meetings were very meaningful and thought provoking. But because I was quiet in group settings, he feared that people would soon dismiss me, thinking I didn't have anything to contribute.

The feedback Bob gave me hit hard and at the time really hurt my feelings. I felt that as long as I was able to have open discussions with him and provide input to him, that was good enough. However, his honesty and willingness to tell me something I needed to hear to enhance my career really paid off.

Bob's mentoring style was not only one that provided hard feedback but was one where he suggested solutions to the problem as well. For example, to help me participate more in meetings, he suggested that I ask a question—phrased as "help me understand" or "tell me why"—which would at least get me in the conversation. I've used this tip many times over the course of my career, and it really works!

Over the years, Bob gave me lots of other advice and suggestions that, albeit right on, were hard to take. I would often find myself hurt and frustrated at the shortcomings Bob would convey, feeling that I had failed him. I knew even then that I shouldn't have felt this way, as I appreciated the time and investment he put in me and in my career. Rather than showing my frustrations, I showed that I took his efforts and advice seriously and that they were not in vain.

Through Bob, I learned that having a mentor offers an advantage, both personally and professionally. Mentors can successfully help you navigate the corporate waters and help you avoid the pitfalls of a derailed career. I strongly recommend you make a conscious effort to seek out an appropriate mentor for yourself, as he or she can be a great safety net. I have been in the workforce for a significant number of years, and

> During the course of your life, your professional needs will change—and so should your mentors.

during this time, I have carefully and deliberately selected many individuals to be my mentors.

More and more women are tapping into the expertise and advice of mentors to help them achieve their career goals. According to a 2011 LinkedIn study, 82% of women agree that having a mentor is important for career success—and 4 out of 5 women in the U.S. have had at least one. The likelihood that women will seek other women for mentorship (as opposed to men) is greater for younger generations than older. Thirty-four percent of Baby Boomers have been mentored by a woman, 43% of Generation X (those born between 1965 and 1980), and 51% of Generation Y (born between 1981/1982 and 2000).[1]

When looking for a mentor, some suggest basing the male/female decision on what you're looking to get out of the relationship. Studies have shown that female mentors seem to be better role models—providing informal fellowship, guidance within the corporation, motivation, encouragement, and advice on work/life balance, job share, maternity leave, overcoming gender bias in the workplace and style.

Male mentors might be a better choice when trying to climb the corporate ladder, offering general business training, advice on negotiation, leadership opportunities and coaching feedback, as well as networking and advancement opportunities. In other words, male mentors tended to help with success in the workplace, while female mentors tended to help with success as a *woman* in the workplace. Since men still statistically outrank women in the highest positions within corporations, women often benefit from male mentors' business experience and their networks of people in senior management positions. Clearly, having mentors of both genders throughout your career is ideal.

FOUR KINDS OF MENTORS EVERY WOMAN SHOULD HAVE

1. Someone who knows you personally and professionally, such as an old boss or a friend, who can help you play up your strengths and offer ideas to improve on your weaknesses.

2. An acquaintance in the industry, such as a past client, who can straight-talk about the industry and give you no-nonsense feedback.

3. A personal friend or relative who knows you well and can offer a shoulder to lean on or an ear to bend.

4. A business coach or consultant who can give unbiased feedback from an outside perspective.

(Source: Bureau of Labor Statistics[2])

Following are a few attributes of a good mentee. If you've been mentored, how did you fare?

1. Be a good listener.

2. Know what you want to accomplish so the mentor can help you achieve it.

3. Be a sponge. Learn as much as you can.

4. Don't waste your mentor's time; make every conversation or session count.

5. Act on advice/recommendations given.

6. Do your part in developing an open and honest relationship.

7. Don't be defensive.

8. Spread the wealth; share what you learn with others.

With regard to the last point, I can't talk about the significance of finding a mentor without mentioning the importance of returning the favor and becoming a good mentor to others. Following are a few attributes of a good mentor:

1. Recognize and understand the mentee's areas of strength and weakness. Meet people where they are in order to get them where they want and need to be.

2. Create an environment that is conducive to learning and development.

3. Lead by example.

4. Build a relationship of trust.

5. Allow mentees the opportunity to take risks and learn from their mistakes.

6. Make sure the mentees understand that what you are doing is in the name of development, not criticism.

7. Remember that mentoring is not a one-way street where you have all the answers, but instead, a partnership where both people share responsibility.

* * * * * * *

SHEREE DALLAS BRANCH

 Let's face the facts: Men rule the world. Arguably, the fact also remains that we, as women, run it in the background as mothers, wives and as corporate, government, and nonprofit executives. I've learned those dynamics in both inspiring and disheartening ways. In reflecting on my career as a woman of color, the truth of the matter is that the big boys opened the door for me, but my girls have carried me through.

I have served as the administrator of a state division, managing a $160 million budget and leading an office of 40 employees in the administration of low-income energy assistance and weatherization programs. This, my second stint as a government executive in a period of nearly four years, allowed me to take a hands-on approach to ensure that every resident of my state has the right to sufficient heat.

But let's start at the beginning. I'm an African-American female from a traditional, cohesive Midwestern family. My parents were married when I was born, and they continue to be happily committed to one another today. They raised my three siblings and me, all girls, in a middle-class neighborhood. My mother (or "Queen Bee," as my father calls her) was the strong, determined matriarch of the Dallas family clan. She taught us to be the best we could be and celebrated our successes. She taught us to have confidence and to know who we were and who God created us to be. My mother's teaching gave me the ability to see women as friends and as sisters. In some ways, we as a community have lost that as a value. At times, I've almost lost it myself.

Though I graduated from the University of Wisconsin system, I initially attended a college in a southern, historically black college in Houston, Texas. There, people who looked like me were working together and making things happen. Their energy was infectious and contagious. My three-year experience there opened my eyes to what the world and my community could be. When I returned to the Midwest, I saw it with brand new eyes. I began to see the way the community dealt with racism, culture and sexism. I realized that there were challenges that might make achieving the goals that I'd set pretty tough, but that they were not impossible. I knew, just like Mary Tyler Moore said, I was "gonna make it after all."

My first real professional experience was as an intern producer at a network affiliate newsroom. The hours were horrible, the pay was nonexistent, and I barely saw my family during the holidays. But it was a stepping stone to what I'd believed would be my dream career. Being a Type A personality, I never looked for a handout. I wanted to pay my dues, produce the best product and be rewarded in the end with getting my shot. Isn't that the American way? Isn't that the way it happens for everyone? Unfortunately, the values that were the foundation of my youth made me just a little naïve.

An opportunity presented itself for me to make a natural progression into a full-time position as a news producer. I did everything right. I worked the graveyard shift and cultivated the critical relations with colleagues and superiors. So when the position became available, my allies lobbied on my behalf—unfortunately, to no avail. I didn't even receive the courtesy of an interview. I was heartbroken. The person who eventually got the position mirrored me in education and experience. The difference? He was a man. What made it so disheartening was that the person making the decision was an African-American woman. It didn't make sense to me.

That's when one my colleagues, a woman of color, took me to the side and explained what had occurred. She opened my eyes to things that my mother, Queen Bee, had never shared but that often happened in the world of women when it came to corporations and men. I was in disbelief: The concept of women pitted against one another was not something for which I was prepared. I couldn't wrap my head around it, and it left me closed off and distrustful of other women for quite some time.

Next, I made what I thought to be a temporary departure from my dream career to a position in community relations at a city food bank. I worked with a leadership team consisting of all women, including my supervisor, a beautiful black woman whose goals were extremely high. She expected me to meet and exceed them.

My supervisor turned out to be one of the best training coaches I've ever experienced. When I worked for her, I thought she was the meanest lady in the world. I'd often have migraines after leaving work and was often under tons of stress. But I soon realized that she was helping to make me the best I could be. She gave me great advice on writing, on speaking, on wardrobe, and on giving back to my community. She also told me that I needed to renew my trust in women, and the time and effort she invested in me helped me to do just that.

She often provoked me to think. She questioned my ultimate plan to return to the world of broadcast news, asking me if the stories I told through there provided any help to the community at the end of the day. She reminded me that every day that I worked at the food bank, some family got fed. Although building a career was critical, she said, helping others and giving back was key. She went beyond the role of manager and supervisor and became a mentor, and eventually I made the decision to not return to what I initially thought was my dream career.

After leaving the nonprofit arena, I took a job in corporate America working as the customer relations manager in one of the largest manufacturing companies in the country. Soon after I arrived, I made a presentation to a room full of the corporation's executives. All the mentoring and training that I received from my previous supervisor immediately came into play. Less than an hour after the presentation, I received a visitor in my office—the soon-to-be chief executive officer's assistant, who presented me with a handwritten note from the CEO, welcoming me to the company. It was the beginning of a very successful mentor-protégé relationship.

Make no mistake; this was a corporate environment with a capital C and was a total boys' club. After being employed for just a couple of years, reorganization had me concerned about my tenure. Prior to formal announcements, the CEO personally came to my office and said he saw great things in store for me and that he valued what I brought to the organization. That sealed the relationship for the years to come.

After six years, however, the time had come for me to look for new employment. It was one of the hardest things that I'd had to do. Having that kind of sponsorship and support from an important decision-maker was something to be valued; it was a critical link to my success. But because it was a male dominated culture, there was a ceiling that I was unable to crack and a culture that I couldn't change. The experience, though, was priceless.

After leaving the corporate arena, I jumped into the world of government, a brand new horizon for me. Luckily I was able to connect with a number of people in executive and management positions who had diverse experiences and offered to coach me along the way. One African-American man who was well versed in the Midwestern way, and who was politically and socially savvy, took me under his wing and mentored me in government and politics. We developed an immediate, professional bond, and he helped me to understand a very important lesson in politics; namely that in politics, things change.

Eventually I was made aware of a highly sought-after executive-level position, and while I wasn't offered the position, I decided to send a thank-you gift of a plant to the woman who led the search process. I wanted to thank her for including me in the mix and to express that I looked forward to working with her in future endeavors. That gesture was the impetus to a mentoring-sponsoring relationship that still exists today. Soon after she received the plant, I began receiving calls and emails inviting me to attend various social events and to join impressive groups. By accepting the invitations, our professional relationship also became a personal one. She gave me a brand-new look at women in the workforce. I've taken from her an inherent obligation to do similar things either formally or informally for women I encounter who need a little assistance, a little access. It's about paying it forward. It's about carrying our own womankind.

* * * * * * * *

MARY

As women, we tend to be natural nurturers. We instinctively know how to mold, shape and encourage. We do it with our children, our parents, our spouses, and with each other. Women are dynamic. We laugh together. We cry together. We grow together. Often, we will help each other in very generous ways when least expected.

I strongly believe in the power of sisterhood. A culture that celebrates sisterhood and friendship is critical to building strength and cohesiveness for each other. We have to not only find that network but be role models for other women.

As Carly Simon once said, "We need role models who are going to break the mold." Whether in the form of professional mentors, personal role models or both, surround yourself with strong women who challenge you to push your limits—and be the guiding light for others who come after you to do the same.

* * * * * * * *

KIMBERLEY NOON

I have been very fortunate in that I have had some very strong, smart, self-sufficient women as role models. They taught me, at a very young age, that grit and perseverance can carry you through. They infused me with the belief that all things were possible—that if I really wanted something, I could achieve it.

My maternal great-grandmother lived until I was 13 years old. She was a strong Canadian woman of Irish descent who came to America as a young adult and settled in Detroit. Her first husband was an Irish alcoholic with whom she had two children: my grandfather and a little girl who died at 2 years old. While her husband was the love of her life, she realized she could not stay married to a man who drank and divorced him. This was a dramatic move for the 1920s. She married two other men and outlived them both. She also outlived her son. She was a self-sufficient, smart career woman even in that era. When I was young, I often stayed with her on Finkel Street in Detroit. She taught me to love math, and she shared with me a joy of learning and the value of education.

Playing Through the Fence

At 42, I am very fortunate to still have my maternal grandmother, Grandma Wilma. She is 90 years old and lives in the same 26' by 26' home in Detroit that she has lived in since she moved to the USA as a young bride. This is a woman who never worked outside the home and lost her husband suddenly when she was 57. That same year, she lost both her parents and her beloved dog. She often says that in nine months her entire world shattered, and she thought that she would never get out of bed again. But she did. She told me that getting out of bed every day that next year was a struggle, but she forced herself to do it. She persevered, and since that year she has lived another whole life that has been rich and full of blessings.

My paternal grandmother was one of a kind. She was born in 1905 and got her college degree in the 1930s, despite having four children. During the Depression, she attended Communist Party meetings, and as a result, she was blackballed from teaching in her community and had to teach two hours away from her family. She was her family's main breadwinner. My whole life she told me, "Never give up your economic independence. As a woman, it is the only power you will ever have." She put a strong emphasis on education and independence.

Finally, my mother taught me unconditional love and a strong sense of right and wrong. My mom is a church lady, and for most of my life I have heard her say, "It takes all kinds of people to make up the world, and you have to be who you are." She lives her faith through little acts of kindness to her fellow human beings.

I grew up in the "typical" Irish American household, where the father is an alcoholic, the mother is a caretaker, and the marriage is usually turbulent. I actually think that, in some ways, this had a positive effect on me. From a young age, I learned to deal with an imperfect world. I had an appreciation for the "gray areas" in life. I knew that failing in one way does not make an individual all bad. I also learned that one bad day doesn't need to make every day a bad day.

Furthermore, I always knew that I did not want to be economically dependent on anyone, nor did I want to be in constant financial chaos. I believed strongly that I could live a different kind of life.

After much thought and soul searching, I have determined that persistence has been paramount to my success in business. For me, it all started with an intense desire to control my own destiny and make my own way. I had almost 10 years of experience in the staffing industry, and I had a great mentor who was willing to back me financially. I was at a point in my career that I was somewhat disgruntled and resentful in my position. I had put all of my energy into building profitable branches and teams for someone else's company, and I had no equity. Someone else reaped the rewards of my toil, and it was becoming very difficult for me to accept.

So in February of 2002, I opened a healthcare staffing company. I did not have a business plan or a budget. I had a phone (not even my own business line), a sublet space with used and leased furniture, a phone book and a determination to make the business successful. My core business was the placement of licensed nurses in healthcare facilities on a contract basis. To do this, I needed malpractice insurance, worker's compensation insurance and liability insurance. All of these were large expenses for a start-up company. What's more, I needed to draw a salary in order to meet my personal obligations right from the start. I spent long days calling and calling and calling. I made thousands of attempts to connect with nurses and prospective clients.

It took three months before we billed a single dollar. We lost $250,000 in our first year of business. My first two clients declared bankruptcy, and I "took a bath," as they say. At times, it really seemed impossible—but then I would think of my grandma, who lived a whole other life because she chose to get up and keep going. I thought of my great-grandmother, who always told me, "Success is a series of failures." I used this as motivation to persevere, make another marketing call, make another sales visit, make another collection call, make another recruiting call, make another quality assurance call, and on and on and on. It took three years, but we finally turned a profit. Every year since then, our profits have increased. In 2009, we bought another company and added imaging to our mix of business.

As I go forward in my life, I still set big goals and persevere until I get there. There is an old proverb about eating an elephant "one bite at a time," and I achieve my goals just like that. I take it one bite, one little step, one task at a time, until one day I have achieved my goal. Oftentimes in this process, I will backslide or fail. But instead of giving up, I get back to the next task and move forward.

* * * * * * * *

MARY

I continue to be grateful for the women who have shared the intricacies and delicacies of being a woman in corporate and government America with me. We continue to work hard to overcome stereotypes. We're often expected to be all things to all people; it's required that we be part of everyone else's world.

There are more women than I can list who have taught me these graces, while ensuring that I remain who I am. While men have given me opportunities, it has been other women who reached out and gave me words of encouragement when I needed it most. It has been women who have said, "I'm proud of you and what you are doing."

EXERCISE

The questions below are based on the philosophy of Charles Schultz, the creator of the *Peanuts* comic strip:

Name the five wealthiest people in the world.

....

....

....

....

....

Name the last five Heisman trophy winners.

....

....

....

....

....

Name the last five winners of the Miss America Pageant.

....

....

....

....

....

Name ten people who have won the Nobel or Pulitzer Prize.

....

....

....

....

....

Name the last half dozen Academy Award winners for best actor and actress.

....

....

....

....

....

Name the last decade of World Series winners.

....

....

....

....

How did you do? Not well? The point is, none of us remember the headliners of yesterday. These are no second-rate achievers. They are the best in their fields. But the applause dies. Awards tarnish. Achievements are forgotten. Accolades and certificates are buried with their owners. Now see how you do on this one:

List a few teachers who aided your journey through school.

....

....

....

Name three friends who have helped you through a difficult time.

....

....

....

....

....

Name five people who have taught you something worthwhile.

....

....

....

....

....

Think of a few people who have made you feel appreciated and special.

....

....

....

....

....

Name five people you enjoy spending time with.

....

....

....

....

....

Easier?

The lesson: The people who make a difference in your life are not the ones with the most credentials, the most money or the most awards. They are the ones who care.

Chapter Five
Meeting an Opportunity
Networking

"Networking is marketing. Marketing yourself, marketing your uniqueness, marketing what you stand for."
— Christine Comaford-Lynch, Leadership and Culture Coach

MARY

Simply put, "networking" means making connections with people. I like to define networking as the ability to grow through mutually beneficial exchanges. There is great power in networking, as it can result in a large, diverse group of people who will extend connections and introductions on your behalf—just as you do for them. Creating a strong network can help you achieve both personal and professional success. Skilled networkers use a combination of business acquaintances, personal friendships and community contacts to help them achieve their goals.

Networking is easier now than ever before. In fact, in our networked world of tools like LinkedIn, Facebook and Twitter, it is nearly impossible not to network. Social networking has expanded our ability to connect with others exponentially. Through these tools, we have become accustomed to overcoming barriers of geography, time zone and access and live a digital life of connection, collaboration and networking.

THE POWER OF SOCIAL MEDIA

- LinkedIn launched in May, 2003. At the end of its first month, LinkedIn had 4500 members. Today, LinkedIn operates the world's largest professional network on the Internet, with more than 313 million members in over 200 countries (and in 23 languages).[1]

- Professionals are signing up on LinkedIn at the rate of more than two per second. The fastest-growing demographic on LinkedIn is students and recent grads (39 million).[2]

- 94% of recruiters use LinkedIn to vet candidates.[3]

- Facebook has 829 million daily active users, 654 million of which are mobile.[4]

- Twitter has 271 million monthly active users, 78% of whom are mobile.[5]

- 500 million Tweets are sent every day in more than 35 languages.[6]

I have heard it said that we are now in an era of more Facebook time and less face-to-face time. However true that may be, I don't believe electronic interaction will ever replace the personal touch. It's important to be mindful of how you leverage both.

Once, in my early career, I was unemployed and actively seeking employment when my husband and I were invited to an outing with friends. It was a small group, and we knew most of the people there. However, the host had an unexpected guest—an old friend of his who was a professor at a local college in Fort Worth, Texas.

After brief introductions, we were seated together at dinner and started to make casual conversation. We eventually got on the topic of my career and, of course, I informed him that I was "between jobs."

As the conversation continued, I discovered that my new acquaintance had a friend who worked in the human resources department of one of the largest manufacturing companies in the city where I lived—and as luck would have it, he happened to know they were in search of a secretary with a medical background to work in their nursing department. We exchanged phone numbers, and he said he would be happy to make a call to see where his friend was on his recruiting efforts for that position. He made the call, I went in for the interview, and guess who got the job? Me.

Lesson learned? Never pass up an opportunity to network and exchange information. You'll find that people are more willing to make connections for you than you might imagine, and you may otherwise miss an opportunity that's just around the corner.

NETWORKING AND ADVOCACY RESOURCES

- National Women's Business Council: www.nwbc.gov
- Association of Women's Business Centers: www.awbc.org
- Network of Executive Women: www.newonline.org
- National Association for Female Executives: www.nafe.com
- National Association for Women Business Owners: www.nawbo.org
- Small Business Administration: www.sba.org
- Service Corps of Retired Executives (SCORE): www.score.org

* * * * * * * *

CRISTY GARCIA-THOMAS

My mother often said while I was growing up, "When one door closes, God opens another, as long as you have your eyes open to see it." As a child, I did not have a full appreciation of what she was trying to teach me. Today, I have a very different perspective on what this means and how it has shaped my own career, along with the nurturing by mentors—many of them women—throughout my career.

As the first chief diversity and inclusion officer at my company, a large healthcare provider, I lead a team and strategies focusing on strengthening healthcare in the communities we serve by better understanding the unique needs of our patients and caregivers. While I am energized about the work ahead of my team and me, I realize this is new territory. I did not go to school in order to work in this field...this role wasn't even in my original "career plan." I recognized I had the opportunity and the right skills and sponsors who advocated for me to take on this challenge.

My career path follows a philosophy my parents instilled in me early in my career. They shared the belief that I could do anything I set my mind to and strongly encouraged me to have a college degree. So, that's what I set out to do. I became the youngest of 32 first cousins and one of only five relatives in my family to receive a college degree.

At the time I graduated from Kansas State University, I wanted to get a job in sports marketing. That was my "career path." The dean of the School of Journalism connected me to two opportunities—one with a television station and one with a newspaper company. With her support, I received a job offer from both companies, along with one from the university's athletic department. I chose the job that paid the most (as I had bills to pay right out of school) at my city's newspaper.

My plan was to only stay for a year at the paper, get some experience and then set out to do what I really wanted to do: work for a professional sports team. Instead, I spent the next eight years at the paper, holding numerous positions. Within the first year, I was promoted to management by a female director.

One day, I received a call from a newspaper in another city for a management position. The call surprised me; I was not looking to leave, and I had a growth plan at my current employer. At the time I received this call, I was working for a gentleman who shared with me his belief that women could not be successful both professionally and domestically. He stated that, at some point, I would have to choose between the two because I could not do both. I found it interesting that he would provide me with this type of mentoring (fortunately, I have been blessed with extremely successful female mentors who provided encouragement on how to balance both).

I received a second call from this out-of-town paper, and a very close female friend of mine talked me into taking the interview. I was in my 20s, and to my surprise, I was very impressed with the career opportunity and the quality that city life had to offer. However, I would have to leave Wichita, which meant I would be the first in my immediate family to live more than three hours away from home. After much anxiety and debate, I accepted the offer.

I remember the first 30 days in my new position very clearly. I went to work, and after a long 10-hour day, I would return to my hotel room only to get on my knees and pray while I cried profusely, missing my family and wondering if I had made the right decision. During this time, I spoke to my sisters and mother on a daily basis for support, encouragement and comfort. My sister convinced me I needed to give it a year. If at the end of the year I was still miserable, I would move home. I never did.

I spent many years at the newspaper, holding several positions. The industry was evolving, and years later I found myself at a point in my career where I knew I wanted a significant change. Once I had made this decision, I put together a list of a small group of people I admired in their professional accomplishments to find out how they became successful and to seek advice on how to find a new profession for this new stage in my life—where I wished to grow professionally while balancing family life. During these conversations, I gleaned lessons of wisdom and success stories and realized it was important for me to find a position in which I could be passionate about the organization's mission. I realized I wanted to run a business and be responsible for a profit and loss statement. I wanted to lead people, and I wanted to be in a position that had a customer relationship focus.

My original group of 10 grew—through their networks and recommendations—to about 30 people, which led to conversations, individual stories and recommendations of what tools I needed to be successful in my next journey.

That's when another door opened. I received a call one day from a headhunter who wanted to see if I was interested in the position of president for a performing arts nonprofit organization. I didn't have a nonprofit or arts background, so I was venturing into new territory. I recognized taking this position involved risk out of my comfort zone from the industry I was familiar with. However, after we discussed the opportunity and the skill sets the search committee was looking for, I was convinced this position was in line with the type of work I was seeking.

In this new role, I had the opportunity to grow professionally, gain the operating skills I sought and learn more about working with people on a new level. I would also learn how to manage difficult conversations during times of change and meet the unique needs of our partners and donors in a meaningful way. I loved it, and I surrounded myself with strong leaders who I learned from and who helped me reposition the nonprofit. It exposed me to the power of collaboration, and I saw first-hand how diversity in thought, programs and people can truly strengthen an organization.

My work led to a new opportunity when I was approached to take over operations of a large healthcare system. I was able to translate my nonprofit management skills into a new arena. I recruited strong leaders to help reposition the foundation by giving it new visibility and effectiveness. Our success led to additional promotions, trust and expanded areas of oversight. Then one day, I was provided the unique opportunity to work with another executive of the company to provide a proposal on the business case for diversity and inclusion. After sharing our suggestions, our CEO approached me to not only accept my idea, but to ask me to lead the program as the company's first Chief Diversity and Inclusion Officer.

As I reflect back on my career, I am proud to see a series of times in my life that maybe things didn't follow the track I expected, but offered new opportunities that I wasn't expecting because doors were opened – and I was willing to see them and take a risk, while maintaining a work-life balance I was comfortable with. I am grateful for the people in my life who became more than mentors; they were my sponsors who saw my potential and coached me to make wise choices and ask the right questions when doors in my professional growth were opened.

My advice to others is trust your instincts, listen and watch for doors to open. They are easy to miss, especially when you are comfortable and not willing to see, but they are there—and often require an element of risk to take. And from my experience, acting upon those opportunities will help you grow and succeed in amazing ways. As my mom said, "When one door closes, God opens another..." You just have to be willing to see and act on the opportunity.

Playing Through the Fence

FAITHE COLAS

 In 1986, I was a 25-year-old divorced mother of a two-year-old and on welfare. I had two part-time jobs: working in our family's home-improvement business and at my own start-up, a public relations firm where I represented a local cosmetics company and a hair salon. I don't know where I found the energy or the time, but I also had a full-time job as a bank teller.

It was my public relations business that brought me to a fortuitous meeting with the owner of a radio station and one of the nation's oldest African-American newspapers. I was trying to line up media sponsorship for a client and made a sales call at the radio station. I explained the project—a poolside fashion show—and told him that I needed a media sponsor. He listened patiently and, at the end of my presentation, asked me one question: "How are you making money on this?" I told him that I was selling ads in the program booklet. He kind of smirked at my response and then took over the meeting. He made his own presentation—which essentially put my professional life on track.

He introduced the idea of sales as a career and stressed that a good salesperson will always have a job and, thus, a steady income. The one part of his pitch that really got my juices flowing was the talk of earning potential: Some salespeople—good salespeople—earned as much in a week as others were making in a month, he said. It was all a matter of how hard and how smart they worked.

He invited me to join him in a meeting he was having the next morning with a national company that had a local office. I went to the meeting and got my first taste of a "real" sales call. He did all the talking. I was learning from a pro, and the best part was that I would get paid commission if the meeting was successful. It turns out that he was selling both the client and me on his radio station. We were both willing buyers. We got the sale, I got my commission, and I signed on to the radio station's sales team. I walked in the bank that morning and gave my two-week notice.

I had been working at the radio station for about two months when I was asked to move over to the newspaper because they needed sales people. The publisher became a wonderful mentor to me. My first day on the job, she said to me, "Settle down, stay focused, and you can make a good living here."

She was right. The money was good, and I made a lot of sales. It was easy and fun. I relished the challenge of selling; I lived for the rush that comes when the sale is made. Negotiating, or "haggling" as it's known in the business, never bothered me. It was part of the game. I honed my skills and continued to develop my personality. Selling special editions was my favorite. Feature sections on Dr. Martin Luther King, Jr., Black History Month, education, health and housing were popular with our clients and readers.

I came to love the newspaper business. I learned every aspect of it—which I had to, working at a small, black-owned publication. Every day was a new opportunity to learn, and I took full advantage of it. I learned layout, design, proofing, editing, copywriting, photography and promotions. I climbed the career ladder; one good job led to a better one. The newspaper became like home, while also providing food, shelter, and clothing for my family.

The experience didn't come without its pains. The experienced people could be very territorial, which made the learning process more difficult than it had to be. No one wanted to teach the "new kid" the ropes, and there was no formal training course. I would spend hours just watching and listening, thinking, "These people just don't want to be helpful."

I learned production from observing, at a distance, those who were trying to get the paper out on production day. These were often late night (and sometimes all night) sessions. I learned the delivery routes by driving circulation staff from mom-and-pop stores to churches—the two most prevalent distribution points. I learned sales techniques by listening attentively to the publisher and CEO in meetings.

Although I often felt like I was on my own, I was determined. I'd practice layout late at night or on weekends. I studied other black newspapers and mainstream publications. Our budget was small, but the owner did find a way to send me to national newspaper publisher conferences and workshops, where I learned the inner workings of the newspaper business.

In spite of all of the intentional or unintentional obstacles, I was able to become part of this world I so desperately wanted to join. I didn't want it so much for me—I wanted it to prove to my family that I could be successful, despite what they thought was my inability to settle down and get serious about life. I wanted it for my daughter. I wanted her to know that women could achieve and become whatever they want to be if they stayed focused and committed—the same sound advice I received my first day in the business. I also wanted it for the industry.

I appreciated the Black Press, and I respected its legacy. I knew the powerful force the Black Press had been throughout our history, particularly during the Civil Rights struggle. Through my studies of the Black Press, I came to appreciate the power of information and ink. I knew who feared and who respected the Black Press, and I understood why.

The business could be cut-throat at times and wasn't without the infighting you see in so many industries. Women trying to lead these publications often found themselves in precarious positions. Too kind and too feminine, and you were considered to be weak. Too direct or driven, and you were "pushy" or even "bitchy."

Meeting an Opportunity—Networking

Many men thought women were clueless and didn't give us the respect we deserved. Senior members, male and female, shunned employees if they perceived them to be honing in on their territory. Despite the age of some of the leaders, a succession plan was never part of the agenda.

But I persevered, continuing to attend meetings and play my role in the organization. I used my network to meet and work with industry leaders, grow my resume and learn more about the business. I kept my eye on the prize and my personal objective: to one day be appointed publisher of the newspaper.

The year I turned 40, I realized my dream, being named only the third publisher in the 43-year history of the paper. But it wasn't enough to be named publisher—I had to perform. I was challenged to raise the bar at the newspaper. I knew I had to make my mark and break new ground. I was constantly thinking of ways to increase the influence of the paper. I wanted to leverage the rich history of the paper and the Black Press to open new doors for people in my community. I envisioned the paper and, by extension, the Black Press, as moving the black agenda forward on local and national levels.

But there was also the real work of publishing, which I soon found out was no different than managing any other business. You're a juggler, keeping multiple balls—in my case, finances, bills, payroll, printers, staff, equipment, sales revenue, partnership building, public relations and promotions—in the air while balancing yourself on a virtual high wire. Every day was a "Calgon, take me away" moment.

One of the first ways I began to make my mark as a publisher was when I joined as a panelist with a radio talk show. I would later guest co-host on several occasions on other talk shows. I continued expanding my role as publisher on public television as the new co-host on an award-winning television program that promoted positive interviews, images and profiles of African Americans.

However, as time progressed, I began to have conversations about leaving the newspaper. It was bittersweet. During all the juggling and balancing associated with my role as publisher, I was in constant prayer and meditation over my future. Leaving was not an easy decision—publishing was all I knew. But deep down inside, there was a part of me that knew my journey in the industry was coming to an end; I had been with the newspaper for 20 years.

A short time later, I received a job announcement for the position of community relations director for a nationwide charitable ministry through one of the organizations I belonged to. It became the answer to my prayers.

* * * * * * * *

MARY

In times of economic downturn, the need for job seekers to be diligent, proactive and creative to secure employment has become more important than ever. Many professionals believe that 70 to 80% of all available jobs are not formally posted. Therefore, those who use networking as a tool are significantly ahead of those who do not.

Developing networking skills does not come easy for some, as this exercise often forces individuals out of their comfort zone. In actuality, however, many people network without even realizing it. If you think about it, most of our conversations with others are really a form of networking, whether on a personal or business level. Opportunities can come in all shapes and sizes and from anyone in your life. The key to successful outcomes when seeking career opportunities often involves recognizing and taking advantage of these prospects when they present themselves.

EXERCISE

Networking builds resources. Resources help make things happen. Roman philosopher Seneca once said, "Luck is what happens when preparation meets opportunity." In today's business world, over 2,000 years later, this is still a wise statement. Use these tips to expand your circle of influence and open yourself up to new career opportunities.

TIPS FOR BECOMING A SKILLED NETWORKER

♦ Prepare an "elevator speech," a 30-second summary of who you are and what you'd like to do professionally. Think about what you'd want to convey regarding your career if given the opportunity.

♦ Practice what you'd say to the ideal person who might connect you with an opportunity.

♦ Your goals and what you want to accomplish should always be top of mind, and your brief speech should include long and short-term goals. If you are not prepared with a message you want to convey, you could be missing the chance of a lifetime to be ready when opportunity knocks.

♦ Think of people you would like to meet and how you will approach them.

♦ "Never answer the question *What do you do?* with a job title and a company, but rather something interesting that guarantees the response, *How do you do that?*"—Patricia Fripp, Executive Speech Coach.

♦ Always have business cards with you and an updated résumé you can send upon request. Think of every place you go as an opportunity to meet people. That way, you can expand your network seamlessly.

- Many companies count on employee referrals as a major source of new hires. Cultivate your personal network—neighbors, relatives, organizations, religious or community groups, book clubs or fellow volunteers. Look to all generations for networking opportunities. Fill in the gaps by reconnecting with old acquaintances, getting involved in board or committees of your favorite organization, or volunteering.

- When networking or connecting people with others, always have in your mind not only what you stand to benefit from the connection, but what the connection stands to benefit from you. Connecting for the sake of connecting is not as valuable or as productive unless you can connect the dots.

- Write down as many contacts as you can and/or consult your LinkedIn connections. Start with three of them, and depending on your needs, jot down ideas on what they could do for you or you could do to help them in their professional pursuits. Is there someone they know (i.e., a 2nd connection) you would like to meet? See if your connection might introduce you. As you meet with people and share your elevator speech, make improvements along the way. Practice makes perfect.

NOTES

....

....

....

....

....

....

....

Chapter Six
Little Torches
Women as Leaders

"If human beings are perceived as potentials rather than problems, as possessing strengths instead of weaknesses, as unlimited rather than dull and unresponsive, then they thrive and grow to their capabilities."
— Barbara Bush, Former First Lady of the United States

MARY

History shows that notable women from the beginning of time have broken new ground, crashed ceilings and changed the world. Some have done this peacefully, and others in a sea of discontent. We are, and continue to be, grateful for them all.

You wouldn't think that some of our greatest game changers, such as Joan of Arc, Rosa Parks, Jane Austen, Oprah Winfrey and Malala Yousafzai would have much in common. And of course, you're right. However, the sheer nature of the changes they've evoked can be traced back to qualities of leadership that were/are common to them all. Whoopi Goldberg once said, "We're here for a reason. I believe a bit of the reason is to throw little torches out to lead people through the dark." Thank goodness for all the great women who have lit up our path.

I believe there is a leader in all of us. Like the outstanding women in our history and those moving mountains as we speak, there are mission critical characteristics of leadership that exist in each of us. Of course, there are many leadership styles, and much has been written about the fact that what works for one may not be right for another. Whether you are leading or being led, you may find it helpful to research and understand each in order to identify which are applicable to you. Having a grasp on the different types of leadership styles, and when to use them, will be crucial in your journey to successful leadership development.

There are several leadership qualities that are more apparent in women leaders than men. A year-long study conducted by Caliper, a Princeton, New Jersey-based management consulting firm, and Aurora, a London-based organization that advances women, identified a number of characteristics that distinguish women leaders from men when it comes to qualities of leadership.

According to the study, women leaders are more assertive and persuasive, have a stronger need to get things done and are more willing to take risks than male leaders. Women leaders were also found to be more empathetic and flexible, as well as stronger in interpersonal skills, enabling them to read situations accurately and take information in from all sides. Female leaders are able to bring others around to their point of view because they genuinely understand and care about where others are coming from. There-fore, the people they are leading feel more understood, supported and valued.

The Caliper study findings[1] are summarized into four specific statements about women's leadership qualities that you may find helpful in identifying and developing your own leadership style(s):

1. Women leaders are known to be more persuasive than their male counterparts.
2. When feeling the sting of rejection, women leaders learn from adversity and carry on with an "I'll show you" attitude.

3. Women leaders demonstrate an inclusive, team-building leadership style when it comes to problem solving and decision making.

4. Women leaders are more likely to ignore rules and take risks.

Dr. Musimbi Kanyoro, President and CEO of the Global Fund for Women, says that as attitudes toward leadership are changing, what women have to offer is becoming essential. Domination as a leadership style is becoming less and less popular. There is a new growing appreciation for the traits women use to keep their families together, to organize volunteers and to make change in the shared life of communities. The newly admired leadership qualities of shared leadership, nurturance and doing good for others are needed to make a difference in the world, says Kanyoro. A feminine way of leading includes helping the world to understand and be principled about values that really matter.[2]

When developing your own leadership skills, consider developing as many leadership styles as possible. As your environment and those whom you are leading change, your leadership style should change as well. There is no one "best" style. Leaders must adjust to the situation as well as to the people being led. Be flexible and intuitive in knowing what style is needed for each situation. Knowing this can mean the difference between success and failure.

As a manager, I find I use more than one leadership style to manage a single group of people. I use the different styles based on the differences in the people on my team. Some of my staff are highly skilled and are independent workers. Therefore, I tend to use a laissez-faire leadership style, a largely "hands off" approach that tends to minimize the amount of direction and face time. This style works really well with highly trained and highly motivated direct reports. However, I also have staff who require a visionary leadership style, which focuses on how the leader defines the future for her followers and moves them toward it.

* * * * * * * *

CHERYL CARRON

Leadership manifests itself in many ways. Over the years, I've found my "leadership stock" (i.e., what I'm truly made of) during circumstances of adversity or significant change, during times when I had no direct authority, and when I've had the ability to influence, guide or impact others—particularly other women.

My own journey with leadership continues to drive me every day in every part of my life. I remember from a very early age, even when I could not define it, that the qualities of a strong leader were those I wanted to achieve. My parents were strong leaders, both in their professional and social surroundings. My father had all the obvious characteristics; command, control, vision, and most of all, humility. My mother was superbly organized, took charge of any situation, carefully mapped out what needed to be done to achieve "the goal," was always positive (even in times of great challenge) and was humble.

Although I was surrounded by characteristics of great leadership, I entered the workforce not really understanding what leadership truly meant or what a powerful impact it can have on an organization and its employees. Through the years, honing the attributes learned from my parents and nurtured by other countless great leaders (both female and male), I've formulated my own understanding and ideal of great leadership. While leadership is different for everyone, there are certain characteristics of great leadership that transcend companies, industries and people.

Early in my career, I was given the responsibility to lead a new team that was struggling to meet its plan. The team did not meet expected growth targets and had low customer satisfaction ratings. I met my new team not really expecting much engagement, given the issues. However, when I heard each of their stories, backgrounds and expertise, I was surprised and overwhelmed. How could a group of people with such a wealth of expertise not be a high performing team? Through the course of our discussions, I learned there had been significant turnover and that this group had been tossed from one leader to the next. With none of the previous managers demonstrating strong or impactful leadership, the team suffered overall negative performance.

Their stories humbled me in a way I could not have anticipated. Each person gave me a new perspective on how we could turn things around and all the possibilities for growth and learning. Had I not taken the time to ask them how they felt and genuinely opened my heart and mind to their points of view (which is a chronic problem amongst managers), I would have missed the opportunity to build a high performing team that was ready to take on a new challenge. In turn, they were grateful for my reaction to them and for setting a new vision of success and a plan of action for how we would get there. Today, that team sustains success in increased growth each month and high customer satisfaction. They are engaged and motivated to continue that path.

Like many other women leaders, I have had my fair share of adversity and significant change. However, rather than focusing on myself and why it may have been more difficult for me to lead during these times than others, I focused on the attributes of leadership that I wanted to demonstrate, and I allowed those attributes to serve as my guide. I remember my boss asking me once if I ever felt uncomfortable or singled out because I was a woman or a minority. My immediate response was, "Never." He was a little surprised, however not altogether, as I explained that I simply refuse to give in or allow myself to think that way.

There are so many things, not just race or gender, that can hold each of us back. If we let them, we demonstrate to others that we believe those things are considerations, thus affecting how others see us. I told my boss that I see every moment as a "teaching moment" (even when you are speaking to someone who holds a senior role to you), offering an opportunity to give insight to others—especially women in a male driven workforce. He asked me why or how I came to this conclusion when many others feel differently. I thought a moment more (as I believe pausing is a necessity as a leader and prevents you from putting your foot in your mouth) and then replied that for me, there is virtually no end to my achievements and I am the only deterrent to my success.

I simply cannot think of a world where others prohibit me. Others may tell you what you can or cannot achieve (the proverbial glass ceiling, look but don't touch), potentially guiding you away from achieving your goals or becoming the leader you are destined to be. Positive and impactful leadership is my goal and guides me in everything I set out to do. I never think of the glass ceiling. I never think of the cultural or gender barriers others would have me consider. I set those to the side and focus on the ultimate goal of being a great leader. It keeps me motivated to achieve more and get the best out of myself and others. Waking up every day, I strive for that goal. It keeps me engaged, and it propels me to inspire others to do the same.

As a woman leading in an organization and industry dominated by male leaders, I have always felt it is my calling to help other women through mentoring. One of the most rewarding roles as a leader is mentoring other women, sharing whatever wisdom I have picked up along the way. Because I had wonderful women mentors early in my career,

I cannot imagine not doing the same for others and challenging those I mentor to do the same.

One of the development goals I give my direct reports each year is to identify one person to mentor and report on their progress throughout the year—as well as what they gain from the experience as a mentor. If everyone took just one person and mentored them, the positive impact to themselves, their mentees and their organization would drive a very different level of engagement. For me, this is successful leadership—giving back, paying it forward and giving someone else the knowledge it took you years to attain. I waste no opportunity to give some inspiration or lesson to someone else if I think it will help them "move the needle" just a little. A few good tips I usually provide:

- Never give up, especially if it's something you believe is right.

- Everyone can make a difference. Always have something to say if you're invited to the table.

- Play the role you want or are aiming for before you actually get it.

- Think of people who inspire you, and emulate them.

- Understand that you can always learn from others, and never forget the gift of humility. Humility helps you see things clearly in times when you need clarity most.

Leadership is a choice. I've spent 20 years in corporate America working with many different corporations in the Global 1000 and working all over the world with different people of varying professional backgrounds and beliefs (values). I've always known that it is my choice to make a positive impact, to stay and fight the battle I believe in. Selfishly, I am trying to achieve my own goal: that ideal of a "great leader" as my legacy. Throughout my career, my journey with leadership has manifested itself in many ways and has challenged me to react differently with every issue, challenge or opportunity. In every scenario, and with every person I've encountered, I've kept the fundamentals of leadership firmly planted in my mind: Be impactful and positive, have the courage to do what is right (but not always easy), stay confident, lead with humility, influence and inspire others to follow, learn from everything, take risks, don't allow others to limit what you can achieve and never forget to bring others along on your journey. It will ensure they lead, too.

* * * * * * * *

MARGARET HENNINGSEN

Little baby tears were slowly streaming down my face. I was crying not because I was unhappy or something tragic had happened, but because my father was telling me how I had failed him.

My parents were on a rare outing for the evening, leaving me as the babysitter for my brothers and sisters. They were trusting me to keep everything orderly because I told them I could. Daddy told my brothers and sisters that they were to do as I said. He took me aside and gave me a talking to, making sure I understood that they were in my care. The moment they left, I went into "I'm in charge" mode. It was a waste of time. The two youngest ones were sort of paying attention, but the other six were not even listening to me. I was mostly being ignored, and threatening to tell our parents did not work at all.

When Mom and Dad returned, most of them were outside late at night, not in bed where they should have been—and I was with them. As my brothers and sisters scrambled to get inside, I was frozen at the bottom of the front porch stairs, watching my father get out of the car and walk towards me. I knew what was coming.

"Margaret, you are the oldest and I expect the most from you. You should be setting the example for your brothers and sisters of what is right and wrong – not being the rule breaker. It was wrong for you to let them go outside at night when I specifically said they could not go outside while we were gone. I'm disappointed in you. Your mother and I left you in charge because we trusted you. You are the leader. That means you are in charge and should be influencing them to do the right thing by example. You set the tone and they will follow. Sometimes being a leader is really hard. You have to be prepared for the consequences of leadership because everything is on your shoulders."

That was the first time I was called a leader. It was 1960, and I was thirteen.

My family was my training ground. I turned to my father often for advice, and it was always the same: be prepared to accept the consequences and expectations of being a leader. He also cautioned me that it would be harder for me to be a leader in my adult years being a black woman—and he was right. I later chose careers in real estate and banking, where women and minorities were not well represented. I was often the only woman and black person in the room. So in addition to working towards my own success, I was also fighting for the rights that would translate into success for other women and minorities who would come after me.

My job with an inner city development project was exhilarating and excruciating at the same time. I spent most of the time trying to convince people that they needed to be educated about the issues facing the black community and then get out and do something about changing our plight. It was 1966, and communities of color were in turmoil. The anti-poverty program signed into law by President Johnson was in full swing, and our agency's role was to get people involved in ending poverty. I was a young black woman, the oldest of ten children, getting a college education and working full time to make things better. If I could do it, they could also.

A year into that job, I met a woman who convinced me to quit and join the staff of another organization as program coordinator. However, the program was in turmoil, and I had to spend most of my time working to make it the superior program I thought it could be. The program excelled, and I loved the feeling of accomplishment I was experiencing as I watched the program go from mediocre to exceptional – social change at its finest. Eventually, I became the Head Start Coordinator for my county.

Fifteen years later, I decided I needed a change and redirected my career into real estate, where I imagined myself being featured in the paper as the realtor of the year. That did not happen. Instead, I discovered that my customers were unable to get financing and my efforts to show homes in certain areas were often thwarted.

When I entered real estate, there were several discrimination lawsuits where women with children and people of color were being discriminated against. Realtors were steering them to certain areas of the city, and lenders would not lend to them. Instead of becoming a millionaire, my activist side rose to the surface, and I began fighting against that discrimination. My battles to be a social change agent led to me being interviewed on the news, and my former boss at the realty company saw the interview. He called and said that he wanted to talk to me about coming to work for him at the bank where he was now working. I hated banks; they discriminated against women and minorities, and I could not in a million years imagine myself as a banker. But he was very persuasive and assured me that if I came there, I would be supported and my customers would be treated with respect and approved for mortgage loans.

He kept his promise, and I made sure my customers were educated about the process of how to become successful homeowners. However, while I was experiencing success, there were still daunting numbers of people being denied mortgages. My city led the nation in denials to minority loan applicants compared to the approval ratings of whites. It was not a pretty picture.

Along with two other female black lenders, we formed a group called the Committee of African American Lenders (CAAL) and led the fight to end sexism, racism and discrimination in the real estate and lending industries. Even though it was a daunting task, it was worth it as over 1,500 of my customers became homeowners. I was now fighting for and positively affecting social change.

On the day after my 50th birthday, I read a report that said while many efforts were being made to lend to women and minorities, discrimination, sexism and racism were still occurring. So, I decided to start my own bank. I wanted to lend the right way—to everyone who was qualified.

Starting the bank exposed my partners and me to every type of bad behavior you could imagine—sexism, racism and discrimination of the worst kind in a heavily male-dominated area. Additionally, we experienced skepticism, from looks of utter disbelief as we shared our vision to people who unkindly tried to thwart us. Women did not start banks and were severely underrepresented on boards in the banking industry as a whole. We were the first women in the history of my state to charter a commercial bank, and our holding company board was all women. Our bank and the lending and retail programs and products we offered opened the doors for thousands of people to become business owners, have bank accounts and own homes.

But even with the best leadership and the best of intentions, things can go wrong—and they did. After being one of the fastest growing community banks in the country and touted as a model for community banks, the economy imploded and our bank did not survive. After 12 years, we became one of the 600+ financial institutions from the largest to the smallest that did not survive the economic debacle. While nothing can change or take away all the good we did, the bank going down was devastating.

After overcoming all the odds and leading the way for social change in the banking industry, thus changing the lives of thousands of people and making our community stronger financially, I was done—or so I thought. On my way to fading into the sunset, I was asked to apply for the job of executive director for an organization that focuses on social change— my life's mission.

Years ago, a cartoon was in the paper. It featured a herd of deer, and the leader was standing on a bluff watching the herd running ahead of and away from him. His comment was. "Hark. There goes the crowd. I must hasten after them, for I am their leader." You can look at this two ways—be prepared for the "crowd" to leave you behind, even though you are the leader, or be an excellent leader and the "crowd" will learn from you and become the new leaders (preferred feeling). A really good leader is often at the back of the pack, because she should be creating situations all the time for others to lead.

Surround yourself with people who laugh at you and with you. Have good mentors, and be very selective. Oftentimes, the ones who disagree with you the most are the best, because they challenge you to think.

Over the years, I have dealt with racism, sexism, people I trusted not being trustworthy, financial ruin, the deaths of my mom, dad, and all four of my best friends, divorce and bankruptcy. People ask me how I can keep smiling, and here's what I tell them: "I have learned how to carry and balance the load of adversity, sexism and racism—anything that can take my focus away from being the best I can be."

My favorite quote (by author Hunter S. Thompson): "Life should not be a cautious journey to the grave, with the intention of arriving safely in a pretty and well-preserved body, but rather, to skid in broadside in a cloud of smoke, thoroughly used up, totally worn out, and loudly proclaiming *Wow! What a ride!*'

EXERCISE

What types of leaders have inspired you and why?

....

....

....

....

....

What type of leader are you now?

....

....

....

How has that style served you and the initiatives you have led?

....

....

....

....

....

....

....

What aspects of your leadership style do you think you need to improve upon?

....

....

....

....

....

....

What is your plan to improve or styles you wish to adopt?

....

....

....

....

Chapter Seven

The 20th Time

Living Up to Your Potential

---

*"In all realms of life it takes courage to stretch your limits,
express your power, and fulfill your potential."*
— Suze Orman, Internationally Acclaimed
Personal Finance Expert

MARY

Perseverance is a day-by-day decision not to give up. What does it take to persevere through challenges in your personal life, with your families, at your workplace, in your community and in your efforts to make the world a better place? It is trying again and again and being able to demonstrate commitment, hard work, patience and endurance.

* * * * * * * *

CHRISTINA ALLEN

I was faced with a choice at the age of 20 that would shape the rest of my life.

I had just completed my second year of college at the University of Georgia and was looking forward to going back in the fall to live in my sorority house and continue my studies in public relations and

---

journalism. My first two years at Georgia I was very busy and involved. I joined a sorority; I was asked to be a little sister to a fraternity; I was elected to serve on the Freshman Council, which was a student-run organization that represented the student's interests, and I was selected to be a Georgia Girl to help recruit potential Georgia football players. So when I was asked by a few friends to spend a relaxing summer in the resort area of St. Simon's before returning for my junior year, I couldn't pass it up.

That summer, I spent most of my days working as a waitress and occasionally at a local supermarket. When I wasn't working, I was getting together with friends at the beach or local hangout spots. One night (July 14th, 1989), I was asked to go out with some friends. After visiting one of our favorite hangouts we decided to go back to one of our friend's parents' house because they had just put in a brand new pool.

The pool was inviting, and I was determined to show off my swan dive. In a split second, that dive changed my life forever. The area of the pool I dove in was only 3 feet. I hit my head on the bottom of the pool and broke my neck, resulting in a spinal cord injury. I was left paralyzed from the chest down. I remember being face down in the pool, unable to move my arms or legs. I couldn't even flip myself over, and if it hadn't been for my friends acting quickly, I might not have survived that night.

I don't remember much of the first couple of days after my injury. As days passed and friends and family support came flooding in, I began to realize that this wasn't temporary—it was permanent. I now started to doubt everything in my life. How would I finish school? How can I take care of myself? What is going to happen to me? There were days when I just wanted to give up; however, this is where I made a choice that giving up was not an option. Sure, I could have decided not to work hard in rehab and depend on others to take care of me, but that is not where I saw my future. I knew I had a tough road ahead of me and there would be many obstacles thrown in my way, but isn't that the challenge of life? Some obstacles are bigger than others, but we are all faced with the choice of how we deal with them—so my choice was to tackle them head on.

As days and months passed, I worked hard at becoming the most independent I physically could become. I learned to feed myself, brush my teeth, fix my hair and write with a pen. I became stronger and adopted new ways to get tasks done. I even learned to drive again.

I had a lot of inspiration along the way. I received many letters of support and stories of individuals who had similar injuries and went on to pursue great lives. I read books with inspirational messages and met others in support groups who faced similar challenges. However, it was in 1990, just a year after my accident, that I received the greatest inspiration and hope of all.

A friend of mine who was working as an intern at the White House invited me to attend the signing of the Americans with Disabilities Act (ADA) by President George H.W. Bush. This single piece of legislation opened up all kinds of possibilities for people with disabilities. The ADA prohibits discrimination based on disability. In addition, the ADA also requires employers to provide reasonable accommodations to employees with disabilities and imposes accessibility requirements on public accommodations. This act provided a new path so individuals with disabilities can rejoin society and become productive citizens and lead independent lives.

Believing that my future was bright, and being inspired to work hard, my next step was to become independent financially—so I went back to school. Since I moved back home to finish my rehab, I decided to attend Virginia Commonwealth University where I earned my Bachelors in Science from the School of Mass Communications. Feeling confident after completing my undergraduate education, I chose to embark on obtaining a graduate degree in law through The University of Richmond's T.C. Williams School of Law. In my second year of law school, I was offered the opportunity to obtain a Master's in Health Administration in addition to my law degree. In 1996, I earned my Juris Doctorate, and a year later I earned my Masters in Health Administration. I was well on my way to becoming independent.

While I was in the Master's in Health Administration program, we were required to complete a 14-week residency program similar to an internship. Several hospital systems and managed care organizations would come and interview candidates for the positions, and we were then matched based on preferences. I was offered a position to work in compliance at a large managed care organization. I remember feeling nervous my first day at work. It wasn't about the job as much as it was about the logistics.

When you're disabled, there are everyday logistics that able-bodied individuals don't have to think about. For example, will I be able to get into the building easily? Is my desk accessible? Are the bathrooms accessible? Will I have to travel for the job, and if so, how far? However, these logistics became less of a concern when the American with Disabilities Act was signed, providing employees with reasonable access. So in working with the company's human resources department, we could find solutions to every one of my concerns.

My 14-week residency turned into a 19-plus-year career with the same organization, now serving over 38 million Americans. Over the years, the healthcare industry has transformed and continues to evolve, which has provided me with opportunities and challenges that I've enjoyed taking on.

As fulfilled as I am with my career, it doesn't compare to how I feel as a wife and mother. After my accident, one of the questions that would frequently run through my mind was whether or not I would ever have a family. At the beginning, I doubted whether I could find the perfect person who could see through my disability and love me regardless of whether I could walk. This person had to be willing to give up many of his own personal freedoms if he wanted to spend his life with me. Fortunate for me, an amazing man came into my life on July 31, 1992. We were introduced by mutual friends at a summer concert. He had just completed his first year of medical school, and I was in the process of completing my undergraduate degree and applying to law school. He is the total package—funny, smart, kind, polite and very handsome.

We immediately started dating, and from then on there was never a moment of question for me that he was the one. The next few years were really busy for both of us. He completed medical training and started his career in Pediatric Cardiology, and I finished both my undergraduate and graduate degrees. During these hectic years, we found time to get married, build a house, start our careers and plan for our future family.

When I tell people I am a mother of two children, they often look surprised. I even had doubts myself whether I could do it. What would my pregnancy and delivery be like? Would I have medical complications? How would I hold the child? Will I be able to feed her/him? How would I change diapers? I knew it could be done because other spinal cord injured women had children. I also knew I would need help. Thankfully, I had a lot of support from my husband who to this day is still holding over my head I never changed a diaper (the one thing I did not master). We also had my mom and a nanny to help while both he and I worked. Now that I'm blessed with two very wonderful and very healthy children, I'm so glad I didn't let all my doubts stand in the way of my two best accomplishments.

Like many individuals, balancing my career and my family is important to me. I have given up some opportunities to advance in my company, but at this stage in my life I want to be there for my children and my husband. Many employers today offer work at home programs or flexible hours so individuals like myself can find that balance.

Now I find balance between working full-time and serving as a taxi for my two active kids.

It has been 26 years since my accident. It has been an amazing journey of discovering myself and my capabilities. I have been blessed with a loving and supportive family, friends, colleagues and even some strangers. I am thankful for those before me who opened up the doors for individuals with disabilities, creating a more accessible world, and I look forward to the advances we will continue to make. Twenty-six years ago I thought my life had ended, but it had only just begun.

* * * * * * * *

TINA CHANG

My father was born in Nanking, China. When he was a child, a fortuneteller told him he would have two children—a son and a daughter. Keeping this in mind as he grew older, he knew that staying in China would never allow his future daughter to have the same opportunities as his future son would have. With great respect for Americans and The American Dream, he moved to Queens, New York as a young man. It was there he met my mother, who was born in Hong Kong, and they married in the 1950s. And, just as the fortuneteller predicted, my parents had two children—first my older brother, and then me.

While both of my parents embraced America and all it had to offer, they were Chinese at heart—and they raised my brother and me with traditional Chinese values and expectations. Their reigns and controls over my life were very tight, which made it difficult to be the strong, independent individual they always encouraged me to be.

Living up to the dreams of immigrant Chinese parents has been hard. They want me to make them proud, strive to achieve, respect my elders, remember how lucky I am because of the sacrifices people have made for me throughout my life, and not waste my life or mess up along the way. The pressure from my parents and the legacy of my family has been greater than any pressure or barriers from the community in which I live—and that is saying a lot. I once heard that first-generation Chinese girls in America had the highest suicide rate of any single demographic. I'm not sure if that is true or not, but I can certainly relate to the pressures of being a first generation Chinese girl in America.

When it came time for college, I couldn't wait to leave home. When I asked how far I could go, my mother told me I had to stay east of the Mississippi River—so I chose the University of Wisconsin in Madison. After graduation, I began my career with a job at a leading consulting company in Milwaukee.

When I arrived in Milwaukee, it became apparent to me that the city didn't really know what to do with me. While a minority-majority city, there was (and still is) not a significant Chinese population in Milwaukee. I have suffered many instances of racism, many of which I believe are a backlash against the Hmong and Laotian populations—but that doesn't matter. People generally think we are all just Chinese. To this day, anytime something big is happening in China, people ask me why (as if I represent all Chinese thought). Once when a US plane was held in China, many people asked me why the Chinese wouldn't give our plane back.

Two years after starting at my job, one of my co-workers and I left to launch SysLogic, Inc. In 2001, I purchased majority ownership in SysLogic and became its CEO. I am now the company's sole owner. I am also on the board of a dozen non-profit and two for-profit organizations.

Now that I have been in Milwaukee for several years, I can say with conviction that the community here has been good to me. I receive many opportunities to participate in community issues. People who are dedicated to growing women and minority leaders often recommend me. However, I can't help but wonder if those recommendations come from the right place. Do I get opportunities because I can really contribute, or do I get them because they need to diversify who is sitting at the table? I still find myself questioning if my voice really counts or if anyone really wants to hear it, but I give it willingly.

* * * * * * * *

MARY

If we are willing to learn how to recognize the many derailers that can often send us off course and impede our ability to persevere, then we are better prepared to overcome the thing that can cause us to crash and burn. Derailers such as fear, joylessness, jealousy and anger are just a few of the obstacles that support or impede our efforts to persevere.

When there is a lack of perseverance, we are not equipped to face the challenges that can cause us to lose heart over time, or even lose our way. When we feel lost, overwhelmed, betrayed or just plain tired of the everyday stresses brought on by everyday living, our morale is often drained and causes us to throw our hands up in total defeat.

We are better equipped to handle these obstacles, and better prepared to overcome them, if we know and understand that we have a choice as to how we respond. Even in the toughest situations, knowing you have choices and exercising those choices are key components in how we persevere. We have to nurture the rewarding times, such as when we experience the joy of working together on something hard but worthwhile, and realize we've made a small difference. Or, as Julie Andrews once said, "Perseverance is failing 19 times and succeeding the 20th."

People throughout time have persevered by facing challenges and overcoming obstacles. We too can persevere, if we know how. The ability to persevere is in all of us—we just need to know when to reach within ourselves and grab it.

Things that will impede your ability to persevere:

- You escape or avoid your problems.
- You blame yourself.
- You blame other people.
- You blame chance.
- You blame other things, forces, or powers.

Recommended ways to help you persevere:

- Face and accept what happens in your life.
- Express your feelings.
- Write about your feelings.
- Get help if you need it.
- Take good care of yourself.
- Learn and grow from your experiences, including the ones that hurt.

Put perseverance into action with the following tips:

- ♦ When something starts to bother you, wait as long as you can before you express frustration.
- ♦ When something doesn't work right, try again and again.
- ♦ Don't lose your temper when something upsets you.
- ♦ Keep working at something that is difficult until you complete it.
- ♦ Don't give up on difficult jobs or situations.
- ♦ Focus on someone or something that ordinarily makes you lose your patience and try to understand it/them.
- ♦ Work a little harder or a few minutes longer on a task that you do not like.

Be inspired by those who persevered despite handicaps and disabilities, such as:

- ♦ Beethoven (composer) - deaf
- ♦ Ray Charles (musician) - blind
- ♦ Thomas Edison (inventor) - learning disability
- ♦ Albert Einstein (scientist) - learning disability
- ♦ Terry Fox (runner) - amputee with cancer
- ♦ Stevie Wonder (musician) - blind
- ♦ James Earl Jones (actor) - stutterer
- ♦ Helen Keller (author) - deaf and blind
- ♦ Marlee Matlin (actress) - deaf
- ♦ Franklin D. Roosevelt (president) - paralyzed from polio
- ♦ Vincent Van Gogh (artist) - mentally ill

- Woodrow Wilson (president) - learning disability

- Itzhak Perlman (concert violinist) - paralyzed from the waist down

- Stephen Hawking (physicist) - Lou Gehrig's disease

- Wilma Randolph was an Olympics Gold medalist in track who was not able to walk properly as a child.

- Martin Luther King, Jr. worked very hard to lead the Civil Rights movement in the 1960s. He withstood prejudice and resistance to change.

* * * * * * * *

EXERCISE

- Write about difficult situations, and how you handled them, without giving up.

- Find out what help is available for people who face difficult situations—counselors, psychologists, social workers, psychiatrists, therapists, life coaches and other professionals.

- Explore the healing power of exercise.

- Explore the healing power of pets.

- Put some extra effort into a project that is difficult and try to improve your skill (like public speaking or learning a dance).

NOTES

Chapter Eight

A New Beginning

Future Women Leaders

---

*"The young do not know enough to be prudent, and therefore
they attempt the impossible, and achieve it,
generation after generation."*
— Pearl S. Buck, Civil Rights Activist,
Women's Rights Activist, Author

MARY

Looking back over my life as a Baby Boomer, I take a lot of pride in having been part of this generation and all that has been accomplished over the years. I have witnessed incredible changes over several decades, each playing an important part in shaping us into who we are today and what we stand for—and why:

♦ In the 1950s, children were seen and not heard. However, rock and roll, along with its rebellious image, brought about a change within this culture. Elvis and James Dean were the symbols of rebellious youth, as was Pat Boone. Jerry Mathers as "the Beaver" was our poster boy, but not all of us lived a tranquil life in suburbia with perfect parents like Ward and June Cleaver. However, regardless of racial or economic standing, I believe it's safe to say that most of us could relate to families having a male dominated figure leading the household who worked every day at a job that he eventually retired from. Many women were stay-at-home moms, though that was definitely not universal.

♦ The 1960s started with such promise. Many families owned homes in suburbia, a young president had just been elected and most had never heard of Vietnam. Ed Sullivan introduced America to John, Paul, George and Ringo. This decade ended with protest, flower power, assassinations and the endlessness of the Vietnam War.

♦ The 1970s were in some ways part of a lost decade—an opportunity for change that was never taken advantage of. The repulsive word "downsizing" became the norm as recession and inflation took hold—and yet we also became aware of the environment and that we needed to protect it. That focus on protecting and preserving our planet continued and is more prevalent today than ever before.

♦ The 1980s produced a product that has resulted in one of the biggest changes in how we live. The personal computer was introduced by Apple in 1977, allowing the management of personal finances, quick word processing and desktop publishing from home. Businesses could now manage payroll, mailing lists and inventories from one small machine. Gone were the ledgers of the past. Silicon Valley in California, home to many of the companies that produced the computer processors, became the symbolic heart of the American technological economy.

♦ During the 1990s, the United States became the world's superpower. It possessed the world's most productive economy and most mighty military. It dominated global trade and banking, and its popular culture was influential across much of the globe. The digital age was well underway, as most of us began the decade without the Internet, cell phones or laptops but ended with all. We prospered, and our culture was alive and well. This decade brought hip-hop, the first Harry Potter novels, *Friends*, *Seinfeld* and *The Simpsons*.

♦ The 2000s transformed us, as the tragedy of 9/11 changed our ideals of freedom and security in America. Its impact had both immediate and long-term effects on the American economy, some of which we still see today. We were a changed nation, and it was a tumultuous decade—but we banded together and made incredible changes. We elected America's first black President, began legalizing gay marriage and introduced social media to our all-time high population of 300 million.

As we move through this next decade and beyond, the only thing we can count on is change. The changing face of America will be literal, with population changes in race, the rise of interracial marriages and the effects of border policy on immigration. Our population as a whole will change, as people are living longer than ever before. And social issues, politics, religion and technology will continue to change and affect our economy and our lifestyles.

Who are we today? There are currently six living generations in America, made up of fairly distinct groups of people. Generally speaking, each generation has lived through and learned from their own set of experiences, which has shaped their ideals and attributes in a similar fashion.

Generation X, by its broadest definition, is comprised of individuals born between 1965 and 1980 (often referred to as "Baby Busters" because they follow the baby boom that began after WWII and declined in 1957). The collective persona of Gen X'ers is frequently debated and discussed among academicians and marketing experts worldwide. There are approximately 50 million members of Generation X in North America (US and Canada), Australia and Europe.

Maybe it was our turbulent childhoods, but Generation X has proven to be highly adaptable to change. They saw their parents lose so many jobs that they learned to make changes whenever necessary to get ahead. Thus, Generation X has been viewed as disloyal employees and/or uncommitted to jobs. In reality, Gen X'ers are committed to their own survival and value work-life balance. They know all too well that the job they sacrifice everything for today might not be there tomorrow, so why give it their all and risk losing their families in the process?[1]

* * * * * * * *

ANGELA BROOKS

I've learned a lot in my short, little life. Proudly being born into "Generation X" has definitely shaped my career and lifestyle choice. Wedged in between 80 million Baby Boomers and 78 million Millennials, Generation X has nearly 50 million members. Our political experiences are shaped by the end of the Cold War and the fall of the Berlin Wall. We saw the inception of the home computer, the rise of video games and the Internet as a tool for social and commercial purposes. Dot com businesses, MTV, grunge music, hip hop culture and AIDS are associated with this generation. The US Census Bureau cites Generation X as statistically holding the highest education levels when looking at age groups. Yep, that's me!

My business aspirations began when I was a little girl. I was intrigued by images of corporate women that I would see on TV, in business, in the community and in my family. Something about the professionalism and poise that these women would portray in my young mind would always catch my attention. I began to seriously pursue my business aspirations when I took my first accounting course as a senior in high school. The accounting field, I thought, is where I want to be. More so than just the pure job description, what really drove me into this career was the fact that, at the time, it was a career choice that was dominated by men, and more specifically, white men. With the odds stacked against me, I was even more determined. My stubborn mindset was pre-programmed: Don't tell me that I can't do this! I'll show you! And sure enough, the more doubters I had, the more determined I became.

Entering college with an accounting major was challenging. The majority of my peers, upperclassmen and faculty advisors would constantly warn me of the difficulty of my major. I was not deterred. However, four years later when I obtained my Bachelor of Business Administration degree with a major in accounting, I decided that I was not quite ready to go out into the workforce and conquer the world just yet. Reflecting on the big things that I had planned for my future, I decided that it would be a good idea for me to go directly to graduate school while I was in the college frame of mind and before my life got complicated with adulthood. Eighteen months later, I earned my Master's of Business Administration with an emphasis in business management.

Both my parents have college degrees, with my father obtaining a master's degree as well. Additionally, the majority of my aunts and uncles are college educated. So to me, it was never a question of whether I was going to college, but where I would go and what I would study. The support and expectation were always there. My parents were, and will always be, my biggest cheerleaders. Everything I have accomplished in life is because of them and the foundation that they laid for me. I was also very fortunate to have many mentors along the way to guide me to resources and options that would have otherwise been unavailable to me.

So there I was, 23 years old, with an accounting degree and an MBA. During the course of grad school, I had become engaged to be married. To me, it was the natural next phase of my life: marriage, family and career. After the wedding, I relocated to Chicago to begin my career. I was offered a position in healthcare administration at a premier downtown academic hospital managing the finances of a large multi-specialty department. I took pleasure in knowing that I could apply my finance background to any industry and was excited to be in women's healthcare. I was ready.

What I wasn't prepared for was what I refer to as the "triple whammy"—I was young, black and a woman! I managed budgets for many different programs including clinical, research and education. I had to stand up and hold my ground to well-accomplished and noteworthy medical doctors, surgeons and researchers. Gaining their respect and confidence was a huge challenge. I would often get comments like, "I have shoes older than you!" I learned very quickly that I had to work harder, longer and be ten times better to gain half as much esteem and value as my (white) predecessor.

I was up for the challenge. I was extremely fortunate to have a very supportive boss, who believed in my capabilities and continued to challenge me to achieve new levels of growth both professionally and personally. Over the course of five years, she mentored me into positions that strategically gave me an advantage for rapid advancement.

Then it happened. She was replaced. Just like that. The department chair retired and the incoming chair made it clear that he was bringing his own administrator. Poof! Everything that she had dedicated her time and energy to for several years was taken from her, right before my eyes! I was now put into an awkward position of bridging the gap between the old and new administrator. I embraced the change, excited about the knowledge and experience that I could gain through this transitional process. I jumped over hurdles and went above and beyond to prove my dedication and capabilities to my new boss.

Then it was my turn. It became apparent that I was being targeted for elimination. My work was no longer good enough. I was given projects, goals and deadlines that were unattainable and obvious failure traps. My work life had become miserable. I had gone from loving my job and career to completely resenting it in a matter of months. The writing was on the wall, and I began to explore my options. I was devastated.

I had worked so long putting my blood and sweat into this organization, only to have it all taken away at the drop of a dime. It was at this point in my life that I realized that no matter how well I had performed and how much I had sacrificed, as long as I worked for someone else, my fate and destiny were in the hands of that person or organization. If they believed in me, I would thrive. If they didn't or had a different agenda, I would fail.

Exploring my options led me to the decision of resigning from the torture of eminent termination. I quit without having another job opportunity lined up. At the time I had a two-year-old son, and, difficult as it was, my husband and I had agreed that we should part ways and get a divorce. Talk about a major life transition! I decided to relocate my son and me back to my hometown, where I had the support network of family and friends.

During this transition, it became very evident that I did not want to put my future in someone else's hands. I wanted to be self-employed. I wanted to be in control of my own fate and my own successes and failures. It was then that I refocused to pursue my dreams of entrepreneurship.

I decided that a good place to start would be looking into franchises. I was new at this, but I liked the business concept of being in business for myself but not by myself. After careful research and through process of elimination, I decided to pursue a pack and ship franchise. It didn't seem that difficult. The franchise picked the location, built out the space, set up my store and trained me. How wonderful! I walked in and everything was put together. The computers were networked and working, and I just had to show up and run the business. I took on the concept of having a family business, so I employed family members who believed in me and my vision. I enjoyed the business, the work, and the customers.

After about three years, and with the support, guidance and encouragement of my family and friends, I relocated my previous business into my own building and began operations independently. Although it is challenging and overwhelming at times, I continue to value the experience and knowledge that I'm gaining through this particular transition. I didn't just walk in with everything in place and ready to go. I had to work diligently through every detail to open independently.

With the transition that the economy is going through, it has proven to be very difficult, and at times discouraging, but I continue to remain optimistic. African-American human rights leader Frederick Douglass said it best... "If there is no struggle, there is no progress." My faith continues to remain strong, and I believe that if I can make it through these trying times and figure this all out, I will be a stronger person and better prepared for life's future challenges.

At this point, I still don't know what I want to be when I grow up. At the end of the day, I want to be happy and to make a positive impact in the lives of others. I would love to be in a position to make a difference through philanthropic efforts. I want to have much so that I can give much. I have learned a lot in my short little life, but I still have a lot to learn! Through education I have created options, and through my faith, family and friends I have been fortunate to pursue my dreams. Only God knows where it all ends, but for now, I just continue to do my part and follow His lead.

* * * * * * * *

MARY

As I enjoy my front-row seat in watching change continue to evolve us, I have my eye on the world's next generation of leaders. This emerging group of workers. who most are calling the "Millennial Generation," were born between 1981/1982 and 2000—and they are a different breed than the generation before them (Generation X) and the Baby Boomers before them.

How are they described? They're outgoing, technologically skilled, and they love a challenge. They often have a not-so-favorable reputation for being spoiled, self-centered and demanding, but I find the truth to be much to the contrary. Their parents' mantras perpetuated a sense of self-confidence and the desire to find their own unique talents. While it is true that this generation of workers expect a lot from their employers, they also want to give a lot.

The Millennials, otherwise known as Generation Y, are the future leaders of our institutions and businesses. Roughly, this demographic makes up about 80 million members, which is a group larger than both Generation X and the Baby Boomers. This generation of Americans will have an enormous impact on the future landscape of the workforce, and as these new employees begin

---

AMERICA'S GENERATIONS

- GI Generation (Born 1901–1926)
- Mature/Silents (Born 1927–1945)
- Baby Boomers (Born 1946–1964)
- Generation X (Born 1965–1980)
- Generation Y/Millennials (Born 1981/1982–2000)
- Generation Z/Boomlets (Born After 2001)

(Source: www.marketingteacher.com/the-six-living-generations-in-america/)

---

flooding the workplace, organizations will need to be prepared to respond. How? By being in tune with what makes this new generation of leaders tick.

Millennial employees will stuff their lives with multiple activities. They may play on sports teams, walk for multiple causes, spend time as fans at company sports leagues and spend lots of time with family and friends. They work hard, but they are not into the sixty-hour work weeks defined by the Baby Boomers. Spending time at home with children and family is a priority. Balance and multiple activities are important to these employees.[2]

* * * * * * * *

Maggie Beckley

It was the night before I was due to give a speech at the YMCA Black Achievers Gala, and I found myself struggling to find the right words. I would be accepting the YMCA's Black Achiever of the Year award for my work as a volunteer in the program, which aims to help African-American students set and obtain educational and career goals. My peers, fellow volunteers who range in age, background and experience, selected me for the award, and I was humbled by the honor.

Equally, however, I was surprised, because at this point in my life, as a 25-year-old young working professional, I still felt as if I should be the one handing out awards, especially to the special individuals in the audience who had helped me become the woman I am today.

The most influential of those people is my mother. I have seen her stand tall and make so many sacrifices in order for me to accomplish all the things that I have set out to do. From my mother I have learned so much about giving back, hard work, sacrifice, believing in myself, and, most importantly, how to keep striving despite what may be standing in my way or what obstacles I might be facing.

During my senior year in high school, one week before my 18th birthday, my father passed away. It was a very devastating time in my life. I had decided to go away to college at Xavier University in Louisiana, but after his death, I no longer wanted to be so far away from home and family. I was also unsure of how I would be able to financially afford going to school out of state. But with my mother's encouragement and reassurance that it was what my father would have wanted, I decided to go ahead with the decision to attend Xavier.

Getting there was half the battle, but the struggle didn't end there. I was living in New Orleans when Hurricane Katrina hit; luckily, I had heeded the warnings and evacuated to Houston, which is where I was when I learned the levees broke. It was a life-changing experience. I was one of the lucky ones. Some people lost everything. I was unsure that I could continue my education in Louisiana, but after a semester at home, I decided to go back.

It was inspiring to see the city come back together and to see the president and the educators of Xavier University work so diligently to keep the students on track to graduate. Again, I saw that through prayer, hard work and sacrifice, and by standing strong in the face of adversity, I could accomplish anything I wanted.

My experiences inspired me to give back to others in need of mentorship and advice. In high school I gained leadership skills, learned the importance of community service and met some lifelong mentors through the YMCA Black Achievers Program—people who could advise me on advanced education, since my mother hadn't attended college and I would be the first of my siblings to do so. The people I met through the program have continued to serve as trusted advisers throughout college and now, in my professional life.

Other's community involvement aided me in getting to where I am today. But there are also people I've never met— trailblazers who didn't let society's prejudice affect their aspirations and who broke through racial and gender barriers —whom I thank for my current and future success.

I am in the early stages of my career, and I have yet to experience any major adversity in terms of racism or sexism or any of the other "isms" that exist in our world. However, I know that I will be ready for them when they come. I will be able to stand tall and firm because of those whose shoulders I stand on. I will look any challenge in the face, not with fear but with confidence. I stand connected, reaching forward to those who have blazed trails for me to walk on and reaching back for those who will need to walk on trails that I blaze for them.

Although it is only the beginning of my career, I have already been on an amazing journey.

* * * * * * * *

MARY

Yes, the Millennials will have an impact on business, that much is certain. Many of the changes they institute will drive our workplaces forward in positive ways. By harnessing the input from this generation, employers and managers can be effective in shaping our workplaces and their futures.

Chapter Nine

My Journey

Mary J. Dowell

*"You may not control all the events that happen to you, but you
can decide not to be reduced by them."*
— Maya Angelou, Poet, Author and Activist

Racism was a natural part of our family's life, as it was for most African-American families we knew. But when we were young, my siblings and I were very protected by our parents and had not yet found ourselves in situations where we experienced much racism directly. Because of this, we were unaware of the prejudices that were so prevalent right outside our door—and our parents did their very best to keep it that way.

Years later, however, I began to realize that certain conversations I overheard were centered around situations my parents were encountering with racism—but at the time, they made sure this wasn't clear to us. Even when we thought we understood what they were discussing, we had no frame of reference or context for that information. Our parents, especially my father, kept us oblivious to the outside world and protected us from anything bad that might be lurking outside our walls (both literally and figuratively) for as long as they could.

My parents sheltered my siblings and me in diligent fashion, each in their own ways. My father, for example, was insistent on driving us places and picking us up, wherever and whenever that was, without fail. While our peers became quite proficient at catching a bus or hailing a cab, we were years behind them. It was not until our late teens that any of us began to navigate public transportation. I often wonder if that's why I have a poor sense of direction to this day, as I enjoyed rides and scenery rather than learn how to get anywhere on my own.

I once asked my father why he was so protective and why we had to be escorted everywhere. His answer was that there was a lot of cruelty in the world and that he was responsible for protecting us from as much of it as he could. He also said he knew that people can be very mean and thoughtless, and he didn't want us kids to bear the brunt of that. I didn't really understand his point at the time.

Years later, I would reflect on how his diligence in protecting us may have created a false sense of security about how we dealt with the real world. One might argue that being so sheltered made us naïve and caused us to set unrealistic expectations for people we encountered, just because we didn't know any better and hadn't yet witnessed reality. One could also argue that if we had been exposed to more of the real world, the reality of what we would later face might have been less painful.

My siblings and I went to all-black elementary and high schools. Every day we walked to and from school, which was very common in those days. We were joined by numerous other children as we made our way to the school doors, and none of us ever felt unsafe or threatened—except for the occasional fight started by the neighborhood bully.

Our teachers were all black, and they knew our parents well from parent/teacher meetings. My siblings and I were well aware that if we did anything wrong, they wouldn't hesitate to give our parents a call with the bad news—which could result in a stern reprimand or even a spanking, depending on the severity of the offense. My brothers would sometimes get into fistfights with classmates on school grounds, which prompted an automatic report to my parents. My parents had enormous respect for the teachers who watched out for us and took care of us during the day. They were like additional sets of parents who cared about us and had nothing but good intentions for our well being.

As my older siblings and I started junior high and high school, we experienced something new: we were picked up by the school bus. We no longer walked to school, and my dad no longer drove us there. The bus driver, Mr. Tatum, had a stern demeanor and took no nonsense from any of us kids. If he reported you to the principal, this also resulted in an automatic report to parents. We knew this, and we behaved accordingly. Most of the time, everyone acted as they were expected to during the short ride to school.

I was in junior high, and my youngest brother Larry was in first grade, when the blissful, sheltered way my siblings and I lived changed forever.

Back in the years when we walked to school, we'd pass other schools along the way. They never meant anything to us, because only white kids attended them; therefore, we never paid them much attention. During Larry's first-grade year, however, that all changed. That year, integration became a mandate—and Larry was forced to be part of integrating one of those schools.

He attended that school for one unbearable year. The kids tormented him. The adults ignored him. He was never given an opportunity to belong to the group. The other children were angry, and he became angry as well. If someone shoved, pushed or threw spitballs, all they had to say was "Larry did it," and off to the principal's office he went. He spent many hours there. My parents were dismayed, and they suffered great pain having to watch Larry endure the sad and shameful daily inequities. My family witnessed my baby brother experience all the pain and cruelty racism had to offer—pain that he still carries to this day—the very thing my parents had worked so hard to protect us from.

My parents decided that the following year Larry would attend an all-black school, regardless of the integration mandate. However, what was done could never be undone for Larry. It made a mark not only on him, but on the community as well. Through the years and still to this day, local news stations interview Larry to recap his childhood experience in the context of race issues and civil rights anniversaries. They ask him how that experience has impacted him as an adult. Larry always shares the same thing—that the memory remains painful to this day, and that it continues to impact how he approaches his daily life. Oftentimes, an interviewer asks Larry what he would like to pass on to others regarding his experience. He says, "Treat others the way you want to be treated, and hope they will treat you likewise."

Several years later, after I finished high school, I started my career as a licensed practical nurse in training at Vanderbilt University Hospital. The racial makeup of the class was about 50/50 for blacks and whites. The ages of my classmates varied from girls just out of high school, like me, to mothers seeking a first-time career.

My Journey—Mary J. Dowell

One day early on, I met a girl my age in class—and we seemed to gravitate toward each other. Her name was Linda, and she was white. We started talking and quickly learned that we had a lot in common. We both still lived at home with our parents, neither had a steady boyfriend, and we shared a passion for sci-fi novels. Later, when we had to choose someone to pair up with for a class exercise, Linda and I eagerly joined forces and became instant friends.

What became interesting and very apparent to Linda and me over time was that our relationship seemed to be resented by other classmates, both black and white. We began to receive side glances during coffee breaks and were often excluded in conversations. Linda and I were keenly aware of this, but the two of us never really had any in-depth discussion about how or why we were treated this way. In retrospect, I think it was because we already knew the answer and that discussing it was far too risky. Neither of us wanted to be forced to make tough decisions about how we would handle it. We just weren't prepared for that.

While Linda and I were very good friends, never once did we visit one another's home or go to a movie or dinner together. We accepted that the terms of our friendship were bound by the classroom walls. While we were both young and willing to push boundaries, we were only willing to do so to a safe degree. Clearly, neither of us was willing to take on the heavy burden and power of racial divide—at least not at that point in our lives.

At the end of the nearly two-year course, particularly towards the end, I was successful in building a broad relationship with other black classmates, and Linda did the same with white ones. We spent less and less time together. At graduation, we gave each other hugs as we did with many other classmates, knowing we would go our separate ways. We promised to keep in touch, and we made valiant attempts to call each other a few times. But like my friend Jane from childhood, our friendship was soon just a memory.

My husband and I married after dating for three years, and during that time I spent several years in the medical field as a licensed practical nurse. The hours were long, and most weekends were spent working in the hospital. Getting older and envisioning a future family, I felt the hospital work schedule would not be very accommodating for my future family lifestyle. I imagined that finding babysitters for late shifts and weekends would be challenging. I realized a new decision needed to be made.

I finally chose to seek work in an office environment, where work schedules would be more stable. As I started my transition from a hospital environment to an office setting, I interviewed with companies that had Monday through Friday schedules. After working in the medical profession, I soon realized I had few skills to offer to an office setting. Finally I was lucky enough to be offered a position as a file and office clerk. My typing skills were not very strong, but I spent my off hours going to the library, practicing and gaining confidence. At first it was tough, but I gradually found some momentum and settled into the rhythm of the office environment.

After working there a few years, I was offered a job as a clerk typist at a very large, well-known corporation. I was pleased to learn that one of the benefits offered was free typing classes, as this enabled me to fine-tune my self-taught skills. I stayed at that job for four years until I had my first child. After my daughter was born, my husband and I decided that I should stay at home for a while and take care of her. I left my job and stayed home for a year.

Though I loved motherhood, I learned I really didn't like staying at home. I missed going to the office and being around people every day. My husband and I agreed I should return to work, and thanks to my typing skills, I was hired as a secretary at a new company. I noticed right away that all kinds of people were employed there for all kinds of positions and performed a variety of job duties. I found that exciting and intriguing.

I liked seeing that a person could do a job well and be promoted to something bigger and better. This, I thought, must be what corporate America is all about.

The department I worked in had several executive secretaries, and I was very impressed by them. They dressed nicely and worked for executives of the company. I remember thinking I'd like a position like that, and I wondered what it would take to be considered. I didn't feel comfortable asking anyone, even though I had done pretty well in my role as secretary. As this was the early 80s, it was both common and clear to me that all of the women who held those positions were white—not women of color or anyone who looked like me. But that didn't stop me from wanting the role or doing what I could to attain it.

After some time, I was extended a phone interview for an executive secretary position at a small, family-owned manufacturing company. I had many of the credentials they were looking for, and the person who spoke with me on the phone was very nice and made me feel smart by complimenting my responses to her questions. I was feeling very good about the call and was pleased when she scheduled me for an in-person interview.

Before the interview, I did my homework and got as much information as I could on the company. I dressed in my best dark suit and made extra copies of my resume. I felt optimistic and prepared for the interview, knowing that based on what I had been told, I was very qualified for the position. My interview was scheduled for 7:30 a.m. and I arrived early.

To this day, I will never forget the look on the receptionist's face when she saw me walk through the door. While I never did meet the woman I spoke with on the phone, the receptionist was obviously surprised that a black woman was interviewing for the position. Rather than greeting me with a "Good morning. Can I help you?" I was met with an unfriendly, "Yes?" I told her why I was there and who I was scheduled to see. She flipped open her scheduling book, looking confused and annoyed. Finally, with a deep sigh, she said, "You can have a seat over there," motioning to an area across the room. I took a seat, and she left the room.

The confidence I'd walked in with slowly started to fade, being replaced with a sense of uneasiness and insecurity. I re-adjusted my jacket, picked up a magazine and waited. It was about ten minutes before she returned. "Whom did you speak with to schedule the appointment?" she asked. I quickly went through my folder and gave the name. "Just wait here," she said in a dry, annoyed and uninterested tone. I sat there for about 20 more minutes before an older, gray-haired woman came to get me. This woman was more gracious than the receptionist. She greeted me warmly and said, "Follow me." She led me to a large room where tables and chairs were lined up in several rows across the room. She informed me that I would have to take a test and that I could be seated.

My first thought was that I would be taking a standard typing test, since I was applying for a secretarial position, but I saw no typewriter. I then thought perhaps I would be administered a standard spelling and punctuation test like the ones I had taken in the past. I waited with increased anxiety, still holding onto a good amount of self-confidence.

She handed me a paper test, stated that she would return in about 15 minutes, and left the room. I opened to the first page, then the second and third, moving faster with each turn of the page. I quickly panicked. The test was completely foreign to me. It seemed to be some type of technical test pertaining to parts, angles and dimensions. I was baffled but took the test to the best of my ability, and when she returned, I handed it to her. She thanked me for coming in and said that if there was interest, they would call me. I asked if I would be required to take a typing test. She said, "Not at this time."

Bewildered, I thanked her and left the building. It was obvious to me that they gave me a test that was out of my (and most secretaries') realm of experience. Giving me a test of this nature was clearly their way of dismissing me, thus deeming me an unqualified candidate. Despite several follow-up calls, I never heard from them again.

As a young, enthusiastic, maybe even idealistic woman, I certainly had my own view of the world and expectations of how it should be. While the start of my career was definitely challenged with an unexpected and unfathomable greeting, it did not thwart my plan or drive to succeed. I was, and will always be, grounded with the strength and support of my family. This foundation serves as my navigation to and through each journey in my life, always returning me to center when intermittent occasions temporarily knock me off my footing.

Today, I look in the mirror and feel proud of the person who looks back at me. One of the greatest joys of my life has been mentoring others, passing on the same building blocks that I use daily—stamina, integrity and tenacity—so that they too will appreciate the person who looks back at them. The gift I share with them is one of my life's biggest lessons: that circumstances are temporary, but the decision to persevere and overcome, whatever the circumstance, builds strength and character that is life-long.

Epilogue

It's been more than four decades since Jane and I sat on upside-down buckets and shared make-believe tea along a tattered fence. A lifetime has passed, and yet I can still hear her laughter and feel the summer heat on my shoulders, relieved now and then by a cool southern breeze and the shade of the large oak tree.

Those were the good old days. Or were they? Like many people, my childhood memories are precious to me and will always play an important role in my life. Those tea parties, my friendship with Jane and those tumultuous years of integration experienced by my brother and my family have served as a backdrop for my life, shaping and guiding me to become who I am today.

Jane continues to cross my mind. I've tried on several occasions to locate her through social media, as well as through traditional means, but to no avail. I'm sure she is married with a wonderful family of her own—or at least I'd like to think so. I wonder how her life has been, and if she thinks of me as fondly as I do her.

My family still lives in Nashville where my siblings and I grew up, and I travel often to visit. My sisters and brothers are now grandparents, and we all continue to experience the fortunes and blessings of what God has so generously provided us through the wonderful circle of life.

On one of my recent visits back home, I pulled my car off the highway and stopped by our old neighborhood. Most of the properties are gone now, long since purchased by the city to make room for modern-day conveniences, but it was easy for me to locate the ground where our house once stood. As I walked to the spot that held our old fence, the floodgates of my mind opened—slowly at first, then catapulting me back to a time I could see right before me. A cool breeze came, and I closed my eyes and breathed it in.

I opened my eyes and looked up to the old oak tree, still standing in its place as though not a day had passed. As the breeze created a dance of shade around me, I reflected on all the special memories I recall with such fondness and how that tree was living proof of how unencumbered life can be. Free from lines being drawn and boundaries enforced, that tree did, and continues to do, just what it was meant to do. It provided shade for both Jane and me, without question, without objection, and without bias.

I thought about how much has changed since those days—and how much further we have to go. I took a moment of gratefulness for the strong women who have come before us, and who continue today, to create balance where there is unbalance and create paths where there are none. I took a moment of faith in our future, thanks to the strong women who stand firmly on the shoulders of their predecessors, poised in the pipeline to reach great accomplishments and make their mark as new women leaders. I took a moment of thanks, for standing strong after weathering many of life's storms myself.

Are there still instances and situations where the status quo remains, relative to how I'm perceived and regarded as an African-American woman? Absolutely. But today we see progress in the workplace and in the world made by the contributions of incredible women. More than ever, women are not only acknowledged for their leadership and expertise, but celebrated. I remain grateful for the positive changes—and I have deep respect for the women who shared their experiences with you and me in this book. Together,

Epilogue

we remain grounded by the women of yesterday, reach new heights with the women of today, and encourage a bright future for the women of tomorrow.

As I walked back to my car, I turned for one final look at the tree, watching the massive branches sway as I tucked all my memories back into place.

Endnotes

CHAPTER 1

[1] The Williams Institute, *How Many People are Lesbian, Gay, Bisexual and Transgender?*, http://williamsinstitute.law.ucla.edu/research/census-lgbt-demographics-studies/how-many-people-are-lesbian-gay-bisexual-and-transgender/ (August 23, 2014).

[2] Human Rights Campaign, *Degrees of Equality: A National Study Examining Workplace Climate for LGBT Employees,* http://www.hrc.org/files/assets/resources/DegreesOfEquality_2009.pdf (August 23, 2014).

[3] Ibid.

[4] Human Rights Campaign, *Workplace Discrimination: Policies, Laws, and Legislation,* http://www.hrc.org/resources/entry/Workplace-Discrimination-Policies-Laws-and-Legislation (August 23, 2014).

[5] Ibid.

[6] Julie Appleby, "Many Businesses Offer Health Benefits To Same-Sex Couples Ahead Of Laws," *Kaiser Health News*, May 14, 2012 (http://www.kaiserhealthnews.org/stories/2012/may/14/businesses-move-to-offer-health-benefits-to-same-sex-couples.aspx).

[7] Council for Disability Awareness, Disability Statistics, July 2013 http://www.disabilitycanhappen.org/docs/disability_stats.pdf (August 23, 2014).

[8] Ibid.

[9] Ibid.

CHAPTER 2

[1] "Family Support Linked to Entrepreneurial Success Among Women," O&P Business News, March, 2013, (http://www.healio.com/orthotics-prosthetics/human-resources/news/print/o-and-p-business-news/%7B2fd58362-e44d-4081-8624-d3d8c925314a%7D/family-support-linked-to-entrepreneurial-success-among-women (January 25, 2015).

CHAPTER 3

[1] Bureau of Labor Statistics, Current Population Survey, "Table 3: Employment Status of the Civilian Noninstitutional Population by Age, Sex, and Race," http://www.bls.gov/cps/cpsaat03.htm (September 1, 2014).

[2] Bureau of Labor Statistics, Current Population Survey, "Table 11: Employed Persons by Detailed Occupation, Sex, Race, and Hispanic or Latino Ethnicity," http://www.bls.gov/cps/cpsaat11.pdf (September 1, 2014).

[3] Huffington Post Women, "When It Comes to Women In Management, The U.S. Ranks 37th Of 45 Countries," http://www.huffingtonpost.com/2014/03/12/women-in-management-study_n_4948186.html (September 1, 2014).

[4] Institute for Women's Policy Research Fact Sheet, April 2013, http://www.google.com/url?q=http://www.iwpr.org/publications/pubs/the-gender-wage-gap-by-occupation-2/at_download/file&sa=U&ei=_usEVKn2E824ggTx0YLIBw&ved=0CCcQFjAD&sig2=GcD5X83XgLrJeqEIL40Lfw&usg=AFQjCNFxZyDRURLEmZ0UbJDf-7GYyEVceQ (September 1, 2014).

[5] National Women's Business Council, "African American Women-Owned Businesses," 2012, http://www.nwbc.gov/sites/default/files/african%20american%20women-owned%20businesses%20general.pdf (September 1, 2014).

[6] Huffington Post, "Wage Gap Hits African-American Women Hardest, Report Shows," January 29, 2013, http://www.huffingtonpost.com/2013/01/29/wage-gap-african-american-women-infographic_n_2568838.html.

[7] The 2013 State of Women-Owned Businesses Report: Summary of Important Trends, 1997-2013, https://c401345.ssl.cf1.rackcdn.com/wp-content/uploads/2013/03/13ADV-WBI-E-StateOfWomenReport_FINAL.pdf (September 1, 2014).

[8] AAUW's The Simple Truth about the Gender Pay Gap, 2014 Edition, http://www.aauw.org/files/2014/03/The-Simple-Truth.pdf (September 1, 2014).

[9] National Women's Law Center Poverty Report 2000-2012, http://www.nwlc.org/sites/default/files/pdfs/final_2013_nwlc_povertyreport.pdf (September 1, 2014).

CHAPTER 4

[1] LinkedIn, *Women and Mentoring in the U.S.,* http://blog.linkedin.com/2011/10/25/mentoring-women/ (September 17, 2014).

[2] Kim Kaupe, "The Four Kinds Of Mentors Every Woman Should Have," Forbes, 10/3/2013 (http://www.forbes.com/sites/yec/2013/10/03/the-four-kinds-of-mentors-every-businesswoman-should-have/).

Endnotes

CHAPTER 5

[1] http://press.linkedin.com/about/ (September 28, 2014).

[2] Ibid.

[3] Ibid.

[4] http://newsroom.fb.com/company-info/ (September 28, 2014).

[5] https://about.twitter.com/company (September 28, 2014).

[6] Ibid.

CHAPTER 6

[1] "Qualities that Distinguish Women Leaders," http://www.caliperonline.com

[2] Kanyoro, Musimbi, "Challenges to Women's Leadership" www.worldywca.org

CHAPTER 8

[1] The 2009 MetLife Demographic Profile: America's Gen X, https://www.metlife.com/assets/cao/mmi/publications/Profiles/mmi-gen-x-demographic-profile.pdf (June 19, 2015).

[2] LiveScience, "Who Are the Millennials?" July 9, 2013, http://www.livescience.com/38061-millennials-generation-y.html (June 19, 2015).

About the Author

M ary Jo Dowell was born in Athens, Alabama, and raised in Nashville, Tennessee. After becoming a licensed practical nurse from Vanderbilt University Hospital, she went on to earn a degree in management and communications from Concordia University. She took a sabbatical to raise two children and upon re-entering the corporate world rose from a clerk typist to vice president of foundation affairs and global community relations for a Fortune 500 company. She is currently the principal of MJ Dowell & Associates, a management consulting group.

Mary lives in Milwaukee, Wisconsin with her husband, John, and she is blessed with two daughters and two grandsons.

Mary has received several community awards, including: *The Business Journal*'s "Women of Influence" Award; the United Performing Arts Fund's "Notable Women" Award; Black Women in Sisterhood for Action (BISA) National Award; the *Milwaukee Times* "Black Excellence" Award; the NAACP's "Drum Major for Justice" and "Staying Connected with Our Community" Awards; the *Community Journal*'s "Our Women, Our Treasure, Our Jewel" and "Dynamic Duo" Awards; the Phi Beta Sigma "Community" Award; the United Community Center's "Friend of the Hispanic Community" Award and TEMPO Milwaukee's "Mentor" Award.

This is her first publication.

Please visit www.mjdowell.com for more information.

About MJ Dowell & Associates

MJ Dowell & Associates, Inc. is a management-consulting group with emphasis on human resources, coaching, workshops and philanthropy. Using *Playing Through the Fence* as a backdrop, founder Mary Dowell is available for corporate speaking opportunities to promote employee engagement, as well as professional affinity groups to develop personal and professional growth.

Mary's discussion focuses on leadership, particularly for the development of women and youth, and is based on her years of mentoring and coaching in corporate environments. With her firm belief that we all possess innate talents that are either unrealized or underutilized, Mary's speeches are focused on raising awareness of the leadership qualities within us all—and to tap into, develop and maximize them.

In addition, Mary serves as Mistress of Ceremonies at various business and community events, facilitator for panel discussions and panelist for various women and leadership events.

For more information on any of these services ,
please visit www.mjdowell.com
or call 414-708-9935